CAROLINE DAFGÅRD WIDNERSSON

CONDIMENTS

MAKE YOUR OWN HOT SAUCE, KETCHUP, MUSTARD, MAYO, FERMENTS, PICKLES AND SPICE BLENDS FROM SCRATCH

murdoch books
Sydney | London

CONTENTS

AGAINST DRY AND BORING FOOD

I've been interested in preserved flavours for as long as I can remember—pickling, juicing, drying, and conserving are just a few of my secret hobbies. Flavours that have been harnessed and somehow tinned, poured into a bottle, or preserved in a jar—that's what this book is about. For more than a year I've been mixing and blending, boiling and roasting, canning and fermenting. I've found sriracha on my ceiling after the explosion of an overly potent bottle. I've fought a war against an army of uniquely stubborn fruit flies in the heat of summer. And I've lovingly fed vinegar mothers like they were my own children. All this to find the best homemade condiments. This book is a love song to these flavourful accompaniments, and a crash course in making them yourself.

You might ask why you should spend a bunch of time making your own condiments. Let me tell you: Your weeknight stir-fry will taste better with homemade oyster sauce, your burger will be more delicious with your own ketchup, your oysters will be that much fancier paired with hot sauce that you've fermented yourself. Store-bought condiments, especially for the Asian kitchen, tend to have a lot of additives. If you're no friend of MSG (monosodium glutamate) you have one more reason to make your own sauces and spice blends.

Many of the recipes in this book have innumerable variations, and the original formulas are often top secret. My recipes are interpretations of more or less well-known condiments, adapted to suit the home kitchen and using ingredients you can find in your local grocery store.

Part of the fun of making your own condiments is that you're in charge of their flavour profile. These recipes should serve as a guide for your experiments in finding your own favourite combinations. If you like spicy food, use an extra-hot chilli variety in your hot sauce. If you prefer your ketchup on the sweeter side, add more sugar.

Most recipes in this book are pretty straightforward. Some of them require a bit more time, and others ask for unusual ingredients. But what's great is that the cooking time tends to reflect shelf life—if you spend a long time making it, you can enjoy it for longer, too. Exactly how long is impossible to say, and I won't be able to give you any precise best before dates. You'll have to trust your own senses: Look, sniff, and taste. If it looks good and smells fine, it's generally safe to eat.

If you're only planning to make one thing from this book, then head straight to the onion powder on page 123! It's a little revolution in a jar that adds depth and sweetness to almost all recipes, and which can't be compared to any of the powders found in stores. If you're making two, then turn to the hoisin sauce on page 59!

Good luck!
Caroline

MUSTARD, KETCHUP AND MAYO

Mustard, ketchup and mayonnaise are three of the most common kitchen staples. You could call them the holy trinity of condiments. You'll find them in even the saddest of fridges, perhaps sitting next to a jar of pickles or an old taco salsa.

They are both easy to make and easy to use. Think of these three staples as the gateway to making your own condiments: you won't need any unusual ingredients or tools, and there are plenty of ways to use them.

Most of us probably have some sort of relation to ketchup. I remember when I was a kid and me and my siblings would always get a hot dog with Slotts brand ketchup during our Saturday outings. I loved that ketchup—it was what made the hot dog. It was sweeter and more tomatoey than the ketchup we had at home. Nowadays I prefer mustard on my sausage. Ideally a sweet and spicy mustard on two Stockholm-style sausages, and a fried egg. Pair it with a small beer, and you've got the perfect Saturday lunch.

And mayonnaise, the queen of emulsions. It amazes me each time that the right whisking technique can turn egg yolk, mustard, vinegar, and oil into silky smooth mayonnaise. But be too impatient with the oil and you'll end up with a greasy, yellow mess that's all but appetising.

MUSTARD, KETCHUP AND MAYO

1. Roasted cherry tomato ketchup
2. Traditional chilli sauce
3. Traditional ketchup
4. Tomato paste
5. Curry ketchup
6. Traditional mayonnaise
7. Japanese mayonnaise
8. Dijonnaise
9. Egg-free avocado mayonnaise
10. Soy-sauce mayonnaise
11. Dijon mustard
12. Wholegrain mustard
13. American mustard
14. Sweet and spicy mustard

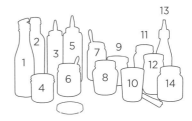

MUSTARD

Mustard is one of the world's oldest condiments. In its most basic form, it's made by mixing ground mustard seeds with some type of liquid. Roughly speaking there are three types of mustard seeds: yellow, brown, and black. The yellow seeds have a milder flavour and are actually not that closely related to the brown and black types, which are more peppery. Historically, black mustard seeds have been used in most types of mustard, Dijon in particular. But black seeds are difficult to harvest, and as a result brown mustard seeds are increasingly used in their place. American mustard, however, is made from yellow mustard seeds.

Crushed mustard seeds release enzymes which produce that hot flavour when they come into contact with water. The reaction lasts no longer than ten minutes, after which the enzymes begin to break down, sometimes creating a bitterness. Adding wine or vinegar slows down and stabilises the reaction and allows us to harness the lovely peppery mustard flavour. If you're not a fan of hot mustard I recommend heating it up. This causes the enzymes to break down, immediately mellowing the mustard. It's also the reason why you should only add mustard at the end when cooking stews and sauces.

You should let your home-made mustard sit for at least a week or two before you taste it, allowing the flavours to mature and the heat to subside a bit. In other words, don't give up on your fresh-made mustard if you don't immediately love the way it tastes. Give it some time.

American mustard is a must-have with the pickles that come as a side to the New York deli-style Reuben sandwich. Or eat it on an Argentine lomito completo, a sandwich with grilled sirloin steak, sauerkraut, fried egg, mayonnaise and American mustard.

DIJON MUSTARD

makes 100 ml (3½ fl oz)

120 g (¾ cup) brown mustard seeds
125 ml (½ cup) dry white wine
2 tablespoons white wine vinegar

1. Combine all ingredients with 80 ml (⅓ cup) in a glass jar and leave in a cool, dark place for 1 week.
2. Blend the mixture until it's as smooth as possible.
3. Pass mustard through a fine-mesh sieve to remove all remaining pieces of seed. This makes the mustard truly smooth.
4. Pour into a sterilised jar with a tight-fitting lid and refrigerate for about 2 weeks before serving.
5. The mustard will keep refrigerated for about 6 months.

WHOLEGRAIN MUSTARD

makes 400 ml (14 fl oz)

30 g (1 oz) yellow mustard seeds
30 g (1 oz) brown mustard seeds
60 ml (¼ cup) apple cider vinegar
2½ tablespoons runny honey

1. Combine all ingredients with 60 ml (¼ cup) water and a pinch of salt in a glass jar and let sit at room temperature overnight.
2. Grind ingredients to a coarse-grained mustard with a mortar and pestle or a food processor.
3. Pour into sterilised jars with tight-fitting lids. Let sit in a cool place for a week or so before serving.
4. The mustard will keep refrigerated for about 6 months.

SWEET AND SPICY MUSTARD

makes 200 ml (7 fl oz)

60 g (2¼ oz) mustard powder
200 g (7 oz) white sugar
2 teaspoons white vinegar
1 tablespoon runny honey
Pinch of ground cinnamon
Pinch of ground coriander
Pinch of ground ginger

1. Combine all ingredients with 100 ml (3½ fl oz) water in a saucepan.
2. Bring to the boil and boil for 5 minutes.
3. Pour into sterilised jars and leave for 2–3 days.
4. Keeps refrigerated for a long time, at least 6 months.

> A blend of spicy and strong and coarse-ground mustard is perfect for making Swedish-style mustard sauce.

AMERICAN MUSTARD

makes 200 ml (7 fl oz)

120 g (4¼ oz) mustard powder
Pinch of paprika
1 teaspoon ground turmeric
100 ml (3½ fl oz) white vinegar

1. Combine all ingredients, except vinegar, with 300 ml (10½ fl oz) water and ½ teaspoon salt in a heavy-based saucepan. Bring to a simmer and simmer, stirring frequently, for 10 minutes.
2. Whisk in vinegar and simmer for 10–15 minutes until thickened to your liking.
3. Pour into a sterilised jar with a tight-fitting lid. Leave for at least 1 week before serving. Keeps refrigerated for 1 year.

TOMATOES

The tomato—the vegetable that's a fruit that is, in fact, classified as a berry, is excellent in ketchup and purées. In this book, and in general, unless tomatoes are in season, I recommend using whole tinned tomatoes or bottled puréed tomatoes for recipes that involve cooking.

Truly sweet and flavourful tomatoes require a lot of sun, and they need to finish ripening on the vine. Of course other factors play a role: the climate, soil, type of tomato, and how much they're watered, for example. But generally speaking you can say that it's sun and ripening time that determine a tomato's colour, sweetness and flavour profile. In countries where the tomato season is short, you should take advantage of locally grown tomatoes when you can, especially if you're lucky enough to grow a sweet variety yourself, or if the grocer has nice high-quality tomatoes available.

Tomatoes sold out of season are often grown in greenhouses and harvested before they've ripened since unripe tomatoes are easier to handle during harvest and transport. They ripen on the road instead.

Tinned and puréed tomatoes, on the other hand, are not shipped until they're finished products. These tomatoes tend to get lots of sun and have time to ripen on the vine before harvest. This makes them sweeter and more flavourful, even though they're sold in a can or a bottle. Since tinned tomatoes are relatively cheap, I recommend selecting a high-quality product —it makes a big difference.

TRADITIONAL KETCHUP

makes 400 ml (14 fl oz)

1 kg (2 lb 4 oz) tinned whole tomatoes
150 ml (5 fl oz) white vinegar
150 g (5½ oz) white sugar
½ teaspoon mustard powder
Pinch of ground cinnamon
3 cloves
5 allspice berries
10 black peppercorns
½ brown onion

1. Blend all ingredients, except onions, with 150 ml (5 fl oz) water in a food processor until almost smooth (the sauce doesn't need to be completely smooth).
2. Combine onion and tomato sauce in a large saucepan and bring to the boil. Reduce heat and simmer for about 40 minutes, stirring occasionally, then continuously towards the end of cooking. Remove from heat once the consistency is slightly looser than regular ketchup; it will thicken as it cools. Add salt to taste.
3. Strain through a wide-mesh sieve or metal colander to remove onion and any larger pieces of spices.
4. Pour into a sterilised bottle with a tight-fitting lid and store in the fridge. Keeps for about a month.

ROASTED CHERRY TOMATO KETCHUP

makes 400 ml (14 fl oz)

1 kg (2 lb 2 oz) cherry tomatoes, halved
2 tablespoons icing (confectioner's) sugar
3 tablespoons olive oil
½ brown onion, chopped
1 garlic clove, chopped
1 tablespoon tomato paste
3 tablespoons red wine vinegar

1. Preheat oven to 100°C (200°F) . Place tomatoes on a baking tray, cut-side up. Dust with icing sugar, season with salt and pepper, then roast for about 4 hours until very soft.
2. Heat oil in a saucepan over medium heat, add onion and garlic and cook, stirring occasionally, for 10 minutes or until soft but not browned.
3. Add roasted tomatoes, tomato paste, vinegar, and 350 ml (12 fl oz) water and simmer for 15 minutes until thickened.
4. Cool slightly, transfer to a blender and blend until smooth. Season to taste.
5. Pour into a sterilised bottle with a tight-fitting lid and store in a cool place. Keeps for 1-2 weeks.

CURRY KETCHUP

makes 500 ml (17 fl oz)

1 kg (2 lb 2 oz) tinned whole tomatoes
150 ml (5 fl oz) white vinegar
150 g (5½ oz) white sugar
1 teaspoon onion powder (page 123)
½ teaspoon mustard powder
Pinch of ground cinnamon
3 cloves
5 allspice berries
10 black peppercorns
3 tablespoon curry powder

1. Place tomatoes in a blender and blend until smooth. Pour into a large saucepan.
2. Add remaining ingredients and 150 ml (5 fl oz) water and bring to the boil.
3. Reduce heat and simmer, stirring occasionally, for 40 minutes until thickened. The sauce should almost be as thick as ketchup; it will thicken further as it cools. Season to taste with salt.
4. Remove from heat, blend the sauce again, then pass it through a wide-mesh sieve or a metal colander.
5. Pour into sterilised bottle with a tight-fitting lid and store in the fridge. Keeps for about 1 month.

TRADITIONAL CHILLI SAUCE

makes 500 ml (17 fl oz)

500 g (1 lb 2 oz) tinned whole tomatoes
100 g (3½ oz) white sugar
150 ml white vinegar
1 teaspoon onion powder (page 123)
1 teaspoon mild paprika
Pinch of cayenne pepper
3 allspice berries
3 cloves
Pinch of dried chilli flakes
1 garlic clove
1 teaspoon Worcestershire sauce

1. Place tomatoes in a blender and blend until smooth. Pour into a large saucepan.
2. Add remaining ingredients and 150 ml (5 fl oz) water and bring to the boil.
3. Reduce to a simmer and simmer for about 15 minutes or until the sauce is thickened to your liking.
4. Pass sauce through a wide-mesh sieve or metal colander.
5. Pour into a sterilised bottle with a tight-fitting lid and store in the fridge. Keeps for about 1 month.

TOMATO PASTE

makes 400 ml (14 fl oz)

1.4 litres (47 oz) tomato passata (puréed tomatoes)

1. Bring tomatoes and 1 teaspoon salt to the boil in a large saucepan. Reduce heat to low and simmer, stirring occasionally at first then continuously towards the end of cooking, for 1–1½ hours until very thick and roasted. You'll end up almost roasting the paste, which further elevates the flavours. Remove from heat when the tomato paste is quite dry and very flavourful.
2. Transfer to a sterilised glass jar with a tight-fitting lid and store in the fridge. Keeps for about 2 weeks. The tomato paste can also be frozen for several months.

Traditional ketchup, roasted cherry tomato ketchup, traditional chilli sauce, and tomato paste.

TRADITIONAL MAYONNAISE

makes 400 ml (14 fl oz)

2 egg yolks
1 tablespoon Dijon mustard
400 ml (14 fl oz) canola oil
1–1½ tablespoons white wine
  vinegar

1. Make sure all ingredients are at room temperature.
2. Whisk egg yolks and Dijon mustard in a bowl until smooth.
3. Whisking constantly, slowly pour in oil until you've achieved a thick mayonnaise.
4. Whisk in vinegar, adjusting to taste and whisk in salt to taste.
5. Mayonnaise keeps refrigerated for up to 1 month.

> I love American mayonnaise, especially on burgers and sandwiches. To imitate Hellman's classic recipe, swap the two yolks in this recipe for one full egg, and use an immersion blender instead of a whisk. You'll end up with a smooth, white mayo, American style. This is less likely to curdle than regular mayo.

EGG-FREE AVOCADO MAYONNAISE

makes 200 ml (7 fl oz)

1 ripe avocado
2 teaspoons white wine
  vinegar
1 teaspoon white miso paste
100 ml (3½ fl oz) canola oil

1. Make sure all ingredients are at room temperature.
2. Combine avocado flesh, vinegar, miso, and 2 teaspoons salt in a tall jug.
3. Blend with a hand-held blender to a smooth cream. Keep blending, slowly pouring in the oil until smooth and creamy.
4. Keeps refrigerated for about 2 weeks.

> This faux mayo is delicious on salmon tartare or as a vegan alternative to regular mayonnaise.

JAPANESE MAYONNAISE

makes 400 ml (14 fl oz)

1 egg yolk
1 egg
1 tablespoon white miso
  paste
1 tablespoon rice vinegar
300 ml (10½ fl oz) canola oil
Pinch of celery salt
  (page 129)

1. Make sure all ingredients are room temperature.
2. Combine egg, miso and vinegar in a tall jug.
3. Blend with a hand-held blender until smooth, then still blending, slowly add oil until a thick mayonnaise.
4. Blend in a little water to thin it out to your desired consistency and add salt to taste.
5. Keeps refrigerated for up to 1 month.

> This mayonnaise is a perfect accompaniment for sushi, yakitori, or miso-roasted eggplant. Try adding some Korean chilli paste to turn this into a chilli mayo.

AIOLI

makes 300 ml (10½ fl oz)

2 egg yolks
1 tablespoon Dijon mustard
1 teaspoon confit garlic
  paste (page 120)
250 ml (1 cup) canola oil
2½ tablespoons garlic oil
  (page 120)
1 tablespoon lemon juice

1. Make sure all ingredients are at room temperature.
2. Whisk egg yolks, mustard and garlic paste in a bowl until smooth.
3. Whisking continuously, slowly pour in canola oil, then the garlic oil until thick. Whisk in lemon juice and salt to taste.
5. Keeps refrigerated for about 2 weeks.

DIJONNAISE

makes 400 ml (14 fl oz)

2 egg yolks
2 tablespoons Dijon mustard
2 tablespoons wholegrain
*   mustard*
400 ml (14 fl oz) canola oil
1–1½ tablespoons white wine
*   vinegar*

1. Make sure all ingredients are at room temperature.
2. Whisk egg yolks and mustards in a bowl until smooth.
3. Whisking constantly, slowly pour in oil until you have a thick mayonnaise.
4. Whisk in vinegar and salt to taste.
5. Keeps refrigerated for about 1 month.

FLAVOURED MAYONNAISE

CORIANDER (CILANTRO) MAYONNAISE
makes 400 ml (14 fl oz)

1 batch traditional
*   mayonnaise (page 26)*
1 handful chopped coriander
*   (cilantro)*

1. Make 1 batch mayonnaise.
2. Blend about 100 ml mayonnaise with coriander to get a smooth cream.
3. Stir to combine with the rest of the mayonnaise.
4. Keeps refrigerated for about 2 weeks.

TRUFFLE MAYONNAISE
makes 400 ml (14 fl oz)

1 batch traditional
*   mayonnaise (page 26)*
1 tablespoon truffle
*   tapenade (page 120)*

1. Make 1 batch mayonnaise.
2. Stir truffle tapenade and mayonnaise in a bowl to combine.
3. Keeps refrigerated for about 2 weeks.

GINGER MAYONNAISE
makes 400 ml (14 fl oz)

1 batch traditional
*   mayonnaise (page 26)*
1 x 5 cm (2 in) piece ginger,
*   finely grated or juiced*

1. Make 1 batch mayonnaise.
2. Stir ginger and mayonnaise in a bowl to combine.
3. Keeps refrigerated for about 2 weeks.

> Try running the ginger through a juicer and use that to flavour the mayo—it gives a bit more of a fresh bite. The same method works well with horseradish.

SOY-SAUCE MAYONNAISE
makes 400 ml (14 fl oz)

1 batch traditional
*   mayonnaise (page 26)*
1 tablespoon light soy sauce

1. Make 1 batch mayonnaise, omitting vinegar.
2. Whisk soy sauce and mayonnaise in a bowl to combine.
3. Keeps refrigerated for about 2 weeks.

> Magic happens when soy sauce is combined with fat. Soy sauce mayonnaise is delicious with prawns (shrimp) and any type of raw fish. Try it instead of regular mayo on a prawn sandwich.

1. Dijonnaise
2. Soy-sauce mayonnaise
3. Ginger mayonnaise
4. Coriander (cilantro) mayonnaise
5. Truffle mayonnaise

BUTTERMILK FRIED CHICKEN WITH MAYONNAISE AND SSAM BARBECUE SAUCE

Serves 4

*1 kg (2 lb 4 oz) free-range
chicken pieces, preferably
thighs, drumsticks and
wings, wings jointed*
500 ml (2 cups) buttermilk
*1 teaspoon American hot
sauce (page 40)*
90 g (3¼ oz) flour
*115 g (4 oz) polenta
(cornmeal)*
1 tablespoon mild paprika
*Peanut oil, or other oil,
for deep-frying*

For serving

*Traditional mayonnaise
(page 26)*
*Ssam barbecue sauce
(page 60)*

1. Toss chicken pieces with buttermilk and hot sauce and season with salt and pepper. Refrigerate for 3 hours to marinate.
2. Remove chicken from buttermilk marinade and drain slightly.
3. Combine flour, cornmeal and paprika in a bowl and season with salt and pepper.
4. Heat oil to 160°C (315°F) in a large saucepan (a cube of bread will turn golden brown in 30–35 seconds).
5. Coat chicken in the flour mix, shaking off any excess, and carefully place pieces in the oil in batches. Fry in batches for about 10–15 minutes, depending on what part of the chicken you're cooking until crisp, golden and cooked through (white meat should have an internal temperature of 65°C (150°F) , and bone-in pieces should have a temperature of 78°C (170°F) at the bone.
6. Drain on paper towel to soak up some of the oil.
7. Season chicken with salt and serve with mayonnaise and ssam barbecue sauce.

HOT SAUCES

Chilli has been used in cooking since almost the dawn of time. Originally from South America, it came to Europe with Christopher Columbus. There are findings that indicate chilli was grown in what is now Ecuador as early as 6000 years ago. Chilli's popularity is partly due to how easy it is to grow—it thrives in most locations without a lot of effort from the grower. If you're a fan of chilli I recommend trying to grow your own to use in the recipes in this chapter. There are so many varieties of chilli seeds online.

I advise you to open a window or keep the fan going when you get to blending your chilli sauces, since the vapours can be quite powerful.

I also always use plastic gloves when I handle large quantities of chilli, and I urge you to do the same—changing your contact lenses after chopping a kilo of red chillis and a few habaneros is a mistake you only make once.

HOT SAUCES

1. Sambal badjak
2. Sambal oelek
3. Sichuan chilli oil
4. Mexican hot sauce
5. Sriracha
6. Piña y aji amarillo hot sauce
7. Sweet chilli sauce
8. American hot sauce
9. Green hot sauce
10. Chipotle hot sauce

A CRASH COURSE
IN CHILLI

Chillies gets their heat from capsaicin, a colourless, odourless chemical compound that dissolves in fat. We measure the concentration of capsaicin, that is the heat of the chilli, on the Scoville scale. Capsicum typically comes between 0 to 100 Scoville units, and red chillis about 10 000 to 30 000. The hottest chilli is said to be the Carolina reaper, which can reach more than two million on the scale, although the strength can vary from chilli to chilli, even within the same variety. Capsaicin levels are affected by both growing conditions and how ripe the chilli was when it was harvested. So even with the scale, using chilli is a little like playing Russian roulette, and I always recommend tasting the chilli you're using before beginning to cook to determine how hot it actually is.

The greatest concentration of capsaicin is found in the seeds and the white membrane of the fruit, so the seeds can be used to regulate the heat. Without seeds the final product is milder, and with seeds included it's hotter. In other words, you don't necessarily need to use a hotter chilli variety to make a really spicy hot sauce. Just include the seeds.

The recipes in this book require different chilli varieties, all with their own character. If you can't find a certain variety you can replace it with another variety with equal heat.

Revitalise dried chilli
Using either your hands or a pair of scissors, split the chilli. Remove seeds and stem. In a hot frying pan, toast the chilli for a few minutes on each side, carefully pressing it against the pan with a spatula. The chilli should become fragrant, but be careful not to burn it. Place the pieces in a bowl and cover them with boiling water. Steep until the chilli is soft and has regained some of its original shape. Depending on the type of chilli, and the thickness of the skin, this can take from 15 to 30 minutes. The water used to steep the chilli is quite fragrant and can be used for cooking. But make sure to taste it first, as it sometimes takes on a slightly bitter note.

Aji amarillo (dried and fresh) 4 & 8

Aji amarillo is Peru's most common chilli variety, and a staple in Peruvian cooking. It's fruity and on the hotter end of the scale. You can find it fresh (frozen), dried, as a paste, and ground. It's an excellent ingredient in fish and seafood recipes, especially ceviche.

Aji limo 7

Aji limo is originally from Peru. I normally buy it frozen, and it comes in colours from green to red. It has clear notes of citrus and a fairly high, though manageable, heat.

Aji panca (dried) 10

Perhaps the second most common Peruvian chilli variety after its incredibly popular cousin aji amarillo. Aji panca is quite mild and fruity with a slight sweetness and a subtle smokiness. Nice in hot sauce or for making chilli paste.

Ancho (dried) 2

Ancho is the dried version of poblano, a medium hot Mexican chilli. The ancho chilli has a sweet and fruity flavour profile, with notes of coffee, cocoa, and licorice. Nice in stews and barbecue sauce, and indispensable in Mexican mole.

Bird's eye 9

Bird's eye, or Thai chilli, is one of the hotter varieties. This chilli exists in both red and green varieties and despite its small size it's got a meaty, rich structure. The fruits tend to be packed with seeds, which is one of the reasons this variety is so hot. I use it to dial up the heat in sauces and spice pastes.

This chilli is also nice coarsely chopped in dipping sauces, or whole in stir-fries and stews.

Cascabel (dried) 6

Cascabel is the Spanish word for rattle. The seeds in Cascabel are separated from the fruit, causing it to rattle when shaken. This is a Mexican chilli with smoky notes and a taste of tobacco. Mild to medium hot.

Chipotle meco and morita (dried) 13 & 14

Any chilli with chipotle in its name started as a fresh, ripe jalapeño. Depending on when and where it was harvested and how long it was smoked over open fire, it's given names like meco or morita. The morita has been slowly and carefully smoked and has a nice dark colour and a glossy peel. The taste is mellow and smoky with notes of chocolate and tobacco. Chipotle meco is morita's ugly, brusque cousin. The meco has an assertive smoky character and works well in sauces that require a deep smokiness.

De arbol (dried) 11

A fairly neutral flavour and a discreet smokiness makes this a nice multitasker. It is excellent for adding heat without changing the overall taste in sauces and salsa. It's also got a thin peel, which makes it easy to blend in both dry and wet concoctions.

Guajillo (dried) 3

Guajillo is very common in Mexico. A mild to medium hot chilli with a decent level of sweetness and red berry notes. Nice in hot sauce and salsa, it's got the advantage of being widely available. An excellent all-round chilli that brings a round, sweet, and slightly hot flavour.

Habanero 15

Habanero is one of the hottest chilli types, and should be used with some caution. Nevertheless, it's got a fruity flavour with slightly tropical tones and does well in sauces and salsas that need an extra jolt. You can find it in yellow, orange, red, and green.

Jalapeño 12

The most commonly used jalapeño is harvested while it's still green and unripe. The chilli is mild to medium hot, with a fruity flavour. Good in salsa and hot sauce and nice to serve very thinly sliced with tacos. It's also nice pickled.

Rocoto 5

Primarily grown in Peru, but there are different varieties throughout Latin America and on the Canary Islands. A good rule of thumb when it comes to chillies is that the smaller the fruit, the hotter the chilli—that's not true here, however, as rocoto is one of the hotter chilli varieties, despite its size. Its flesh is thick and juicy, and the taste is fruity and aromatic.

Spanish pepper 1

This is really a collective name for a bunch of different types of chilli, such as long red chilli, pepper, 'regular chilli', and habanero. The Latin name is Capsicum annuum. You can find Spanish pepper in green, yellow, orange, and red, indicating different levels of ripeness in the same type of fruit.

See image on next spread.

AMERICAN HOT SAUCE

makes 600ml (21 fl oz)

*500 g (1 lb 2 oz) long red
  chillies, split and coarsely
  chopped*
10 g (¼ oz) bird's-eye chilli
*500 ml (2 cups) apple cider
  vinegar*

1. Blend chilli and vinegar until coarsely chopped and combined. Pour into a sterilised jar and cover with muslin (cheesecloth).
2. Leave at room temperature, out of direct sunlight, for 6 weeks to ferment, removing any mould that forms.
3. After 6 weeks, transfer to a saucepan. Add 1 tablespoon salt, bring to the boil, then reduce heat and simmer for 3–4 minutes.
4. Cool slightly, then transfer to a blender and blend until as smooth as possible. Pass through a muslin (cheesecloth) or fine sieve.
5. Pour into sterilised bottle. If possible, let hot sauce sit for 1-2 weeks before serving. Hot sauce will keep, for at least 1 year. It's best kept in the fridge. Try it with oysters.

> The advantage of making your own hot sauce is that you can decide the heat and flavour profile. For an even hotter sauce, swap some of the red chilli for a stronger chilli variety, such as bird's eye or habanero. To get as close to the American original as possible, try growing your own Tabasco peppers from seed. You can buy them in well-stocked nurseries or online.

CHIPOTLE HOT SAUCE

makes 600 ml (21 fl oz)

3 dried chipotle morita chillies
1 dried chipotle chilli
1 dried ancho chilli
500 g (1 lb 2 oz) long red chillies, cored, seeds removed and coarsely chopped
1 ripe pear
1 tablespoon whey, from live plain yoghurt
1 tablespoon apple cider vinegar

1. Toast the dried chillies in a hot, dry frying pan for about 30 seconds each side until fragrant.
2. Bring 500 ml (2 cups) water to the boil in a saucepan, remove pan from heat and add the toasted chillies. Steep for 20 minutes.
3. Remove chillies and reserve water. Remove seeds from chillies, cut off stems, and coarsely chop the flesh.
4. Coarsely chop the fresh chilli and core and coarsely chop the pear.
5. Combine soaked and fresh chillies and pear in a blender and blend to a coarse mass. Combine with whey, vinegar, and 200 ml (7 fl oz) reserved chilli water.
6. Transfer mixture to a sterilised glass jar and cover with a muslin (cheesecloth). Leave at room temperature, out of direct sunlight, for 5 days to ferment, removing any mould that forms.
7. Place chilli mixture in a saucepan. Add ½ teaspoon salt, bring to the boil, reduce heat and simmer for 5 minutes.
8. Transfer to a blender and blend until as smooth as possible. Pass through a muslin (cheesecloth) or a sieve, then pour into a sterilised bottle.
9. Hot sauce will keep for about 6 months. It's best stored in the fridge. Try a few drops on a burger or in a Bloody Mary for a new twist.

PINA Y AJI AMARILLO HOT SAUCE

makes 600 ml (21 fl oz)

½ brown onion, finely chopped
150 g (5½ oz) aji amarillo, cored, seeds removed and finely chopped
50 g (1¾ oz) aji limo, cored, seeds removed and finely chopped
1 habanero chilli, cored, seeds removed and finely chopped
200 g (7 oz) fresh pineapple, peeled and coarsely chopped
2½ tablespoons white vinegar

1. Combine onion, chillies, pineapple and vinegar in a saucepan with 200 ml (7 fl oz) water and ½ teaspoon salt. Bring to the boil, reduce heat and simmer for 5 minutes.
2. Transfer to a blender and blend until as smooth as possible. Pass through a sieve and pour into sterilised bottles. Hot sauce will keep refrigerated for a few weeks.

This sauce takes inspiration from Latin America, or Peru more precisely. Aji amarillo is often served with ceviche, a Peruvian classic, or grilled guinea pig. I've unfortunately not yet tried guinea pig, but I highly recommend a few drops of the sauce with ceviche. You can also try swapping the habanero for half a rocoto chilli to make a really hot and interesting hot sauce with even more of a Peruvian touch. I don't know that pineapple is particularly Peruvian, but I like the combination of fruity pineapple and yellow chilli.

MEXICAN HOT SAUCE

makes 500 ml (2 cups)

2 dried guajillo chillies
1 dried cascabel chilli
*1 red capsicum (pepper),
  cored, seeds removed and
  coarsely chopped*
*200 g (7 oz) long red chillies,
  cored, seeds removed and
  coarsely chopped*
*1 habanero chilli, cored,
  seeds removed and
  coarsely chopped*
*200 ml (7 fl oz) apple cider
  vinegar*
2 teaspoons ground cumin
1½ teaspoons mild paprika
½ teaspoon ground ginger
*1 teaspoon ground coriander
  seeds*

1. Toast dried chillies in a hot, dry frying pan for about 15 seconds each side until fragrant. Soak in a bowl of water for about 20 minutes. Cut off stems and remove seeds.
2. Combine soaked chillies in a saucepan with remaining ingredients, 300 ml (10½ fl oz) water and 1½ teaspoons salt, bring to the boil and simmer for 10 minutes or until capsicum is soft.
3. Cool slightly, transfer to a blender and blend until as smooth as possible.
4. Pass sauce through a coarse sieve or a metal colander and pour into a sterilised bottle.
5. Hot sauce will keep refrigerated for at least 1 month.

> Mexican hot sauce can give a jolt to almost any meal. It's particularly tasty on huevos rancheros, or any and all egg recipes for that matter, and Mexican food in general.

GREEN HOT SAUCE

makes 700 ml (24 fl oz)

*500 g (1 lb 2 oz) long green
  chillies*
1 tablespoon salt flakes
*600 ml (21 fl oz) apple cider
  vinegar*

1. Blend the chilli in a blender to make a paste, then add salt. Place the mixture in a sterilised glass jar and cover with muslin (cheesecloth).
2. Leave at room temperature out of direct sunlight for 3–4 days to ferment, removing any mould that forms.
3. Place chilli mixture in a saucepan, bring to the boil and boil for 1 minute or so.
4. Add vinegar, transfer to a blender and blend until as smooth as possible. Pass through a coarse sieve.
5. Pour into a sterilised bottle. Keeps refrigerated for at least 6 months.

> This sauce easily forms mould as it ferments, so be diligent about checking every day to remove any mould, especially in the summer. If this leads you to discard too much of the chilli paste you can weigh it at the last stage and add vinegar by 125 ml (½ cup) per 100 g (3½ oz) chilli paste.

STIR-FRIED BLUE SWIMMER CRAB WITH SAMBAL BADJAK

serves 4 people

1 kg (2 lb 2 oz) fresh or frozen blue swimmer crab, cut in half
1 tablespoon neutral oil, such as canola or peanut oil
2 tablespoons sambal badjak (page 46)
2 tablespoons fish sauce
1 bunch coriander (cilantro), coarsely chopped
5 spring onions (scallions), cut into thin matchsticks

1. If using frozen crabs, thaw in a tray in the fridge overnight. Pour off excess water and dry with paper towel before using. If using fresh crabs, remove feathery grey gills and innards before using.
2. Heat oil in a wok over high heat. Add crab and stir-fry for 2–3 minutes until starting to change colour.
3. Add sambal badjak, fish sauce and 1 tablespoon water and season to taste. Cook, tossing occasionally, for 3–5 minutes or until the shell is red and the meat white.
4. Transfer to a plate and top with coriander and spring onion.
5. Eat with your hands, accessing the meat with a shellfish fork. This can be served as a starter, or a main with rice.

Blue swimmer crab is a variety of crab fished in the Pacific and Indian Oceans. It's especially popular in Australia. It's a bit tricky to eat but has lots of meat. If you can't find it fresh it can be bought frozen at select Asian grocery stores. Thaw overnight in the fridge before using.

SAMBAL OELEK

makes 60 ml (2 fl oz)

*70 g (2½ oz) long red chillies,
   cored, seeds removed
   and coarsely chopped*
½ tablespoon lime juice

1. Combine chilli and a pinch of salt flakes in a mortar and crush with a pestle to a coarse paste. Add lime juice and transfer to a sterilised glass jar.
2. Sambal will keep refrigerated for at least 1 week. It can be used instead of fresh chilli in Asian recipes.

Sambal oelek hails from Indonesia, where it's served with most meals. It's common for Indonesian households to make their own sambal oelek with a mortar and pestle. You can simplify things by blending the paste instead, but I find the taste improves when it's pounded rather than blended. For more heat, leave the chilli seeds in.

SAMBAL BADJAK

makes 150 ml (5 fl oz)

6 shallots, finely chopped
*5 garlic cloves, finely
   chopped*
*2 tablespoons canola or
   peanut oil*
1 teaspoon shrimp paste
*300 ml (10½ fl oz) sambal
   oelek (see above)*
1 lemongrass stem, crushed
1 kaffir lime leaf
1 teaspoon raw sugar

1. Heat oil in a large saucepan over medium heat. Add onion, garlic and oil and cook, stirring, for 5 minutes or until soft, but not coloured.
2. Add shrimp paste and sambal oelek. Keep frying, stirring frequently so it doesn't burn, for about 20 minutes. The paste should be dark red and fairly dry. If it's sticking to the pan too much, or if it seems too dry, add a little more oil or a tablespoon or so of water.
3. Add lemongrass, lime leaf, and sugar. Cook, stirring, for another 20 minutes or until a thick, dark red paste.
4. Remove lemongrass and lime leaf and transfer the hot chilli paste to a sterilised jar with tight-fitting lid.
5. Sambal badjak will keep refrigerated for a few months.

This recipe is from a friend's mum, who grew up in Indonesia. It was passed down to her from her mum. The original recipe is for a sambal with seeds, which is spicier, but that's a question of taste. Sambal badjak is nice in a variety of recipes. I'm particularly fond of serving a large dollop with fried rice or seafood. Shrimp paste is available from Asian grocers.

SRIRACHA

makes 300 ml (10½ fl oz)

300 g (10½ oz) long red chillies, cored and seeds removed
50 g (1¾ oz) garlic (about 5 cloves)
1 teaspoon salt
1 tablespoon white vinegar
½ tablespoon fish sauce
½ tablespoon palm sugar (jaggery)

1. Blend all ingredients and 100 ml (3½ fl oz) water in a blender to a wet, coarse mass. It shouldn't be smooth, but look more like a porridge.
2. Transfer to a sterilised glass jar and cover with muslin (cheesecloth). Leave out of direct sunlight at room temperature for 5 days to ferment, removing any mould that forms.
3. Place chilli mixture in a saucepan, bring to the boil and simmer for 2–3 minutes.
4. Cool slightly, then transfer to a blender and blend until a smooth sauce. You may need to add a little water to help the sauce become really smooth.
5. Pour into a sterilised glass jar. If possible, let sit for another day to ferment.
6. Sriracha will keep refrigerated for at least 6 months.

Sriracha is incredibly popular, especially in the United States where it has something of a cult status. The original is said to hail from Thailand, but most famous is the Rooster Sauce variety, created by Huy Fong Foods in California, with the iconic rooster on the bottle. It's commonly held that sriracha can be eaten with anything. My favourite is on eggs. Try swapping red chillies for other varieties to mix things up.

SWEET CHILLI SAUCE

makes 1 litre (4 cups)

500 g (1 lb 2 oz) long red chillies, cored, seeds removed and coarsely chopped
3 garlic cloves, coarsely chopped
350 ml (12 fl oz) white vinegar
500 g (1 lb 2 oz) white sugar

1. Place all ingredients in a blender with 350 ml (12 fl oz) water and blend to a sauce still with a bit of structure—don't make it too smooth.
2. Pour sauce into a heavy-based saucepan and bring to the boil. Reduce heat and simmer, stirring occasionally, for about 35–40 minutes until sauce thickened.
3. Pour into sterilised bottles with tight-fitting lids. Sweet chilli sauce will keep refrigerated for a few months.

SICHUAN CHILLI OIL

makes 500 ml (17 fl oz)

700 ml (24 fl oz) canola or peanut oil
½ tablespoon coriander seeds
2 star anise
6 cardamom pods
2 black cardamom pods
1 cinnamon stick
3 garlic cloves
1 x 3 cm piece ginger, peeled and coarsely chopped
150 g (5½ oz) dried long red chillies
2 tablespoons Sichuan peppercorns

1. Heat oil in a saucepan to 110°C (225°F).
2. Meanwhile, toast the spices, except dried chillies and Sichuan peppercorns, in a hot, dry frying pan. Pound them coarsely with a mortar and pestle as you wait for the oil to heat.
3. Add spices, garlic, and ginger to the hot oil and boil for about 10 minutes until the oil is very fragrant.
4. Remove stems from dried chillies, shake out the seeds, and crush what's left with a mortar and pestle. Place chilli, Sichuan pepper, and 1 teaspoon salt in a glass jar. Strain the hot oil into the jar, discarding spices, garlic and ginger.
5. Let the oil sit for at least 3 hours, or ideally overnight, before serving.

> This chilli-rich oil is a common ingredient and condiment in the Sichuan kitchen. It's extra tasty with dumplings, combined with black vinegar. A tip is to take about 200–300 ml (7–10½ fl oz) of the oil and sift it through a coffee filter. This way you'll have both a clean chilli oil and a coarser Sichuan oil.

WORLD-FAMOUS SAUCES

Stored in your fridge or pantry, these flavourful sauces from all around the world will perk up even the most drab meal. Many of them are the secret ingredients in your favourite foods—it might even be the sauce that makes the recipe, as is the case with hoisin sauce in Peking duck, or bulgogi marinade for Korean barbecue. Or Worcestershire sauce, which is guaranteed to take your béarnaise sauce to a new level. The recipes in this chapter are sourced from all corners of the world, and some of them have long ingredient lists that can be tricky to procure, but they are all quite easy to make.

Most sauces have innumerable versions, and their original recipe can be a closely guarded secret, as with Worcestershire sauce. According to legend (which might just be a marketing ploy), the sauce was created in 1835 after Lord Sandys, the British Governor in Bengal at the time, hired chemists John Wheeley Lea and William Henry Perrins to recreate a sauce he'd come across in the province. Lea and Perrins weren't particularly happy with their concoction, but they nevertheless kept a barrel and put it to the side. When they opened it again a while later they found that it had fermented, adding a pleasant flavour to the sauce. This version was brought to market in 1837. Several manufacturers began to sell similar sauces under the same name, which led Lea and Perrins to sue Holbrooks, a Birmingham competitor, in an attempt to patent the name Worcestershire Sauce. The court decided that the name could be used by anyone, but Lea and Perrins held the right to call their sauce 'Original and Genuine'.

The pages that follow contain my own interpretations of recipes I've collected over several years. At times I may have strayed from the original to accommodate the restrictions of a home kitchen, or substituted the ingredients for ones that are easier to find, but none of these adaptations compromise on flavour.

WORLD-FAMOUS SAUCES

1. Bulgogi barbecue sauce
2. American barbecue sauce
3. Worcestershire sauce
4. Chimichurri
5. Plum sauce
6. Pebre
7. Ponzu sauce
8. Taco salsa
9. Teriyaki sauce
10. Hoisin sauce
11. Salsa Lizano
12. Ssam barbecue sauce
13. Oyster sauce
14. English brown sauce
15. Mushroom soy sauce

WORCESTERSHIRE SAUCE

makes 300 ml (10½ fl oz)

200 ml (7 fl oz) white vinegar
100 ml (3½ fl oz) molasses
100 ml (3½ fl oz) light soy sauce
2½ tablespoons tamarind purée
2 tablespoons yellow mustard seeds
1 teaspoon whole black peppercorns
10 cloves
½ teaspoon North Indian Curry Powder (page 116)
5 cardamom pods
3 dried red chillies
3 anchovies, chopped
2 garlic cloves, chopped
1 cinnamon stick, chopped
1 brown onion, chopped
1 x 3 cm piece ginger, grated
50 g (1¾ oz) white sugar

1. Combine all ingredients, except sugar, in a saucepan. Add 2 teaspoons salt, bring to the boil, reduce to a simmer and simmer for 10 minutes until reduced.
2. In another saucepan, caramelise the sugar over medium heat, swirling occasionally, until it begins to darken. Add the sauce and boil for 5 minutes or until thickened.
3. Pour into a sterilised glass jar with a tight-fitting lid and refrigerate for 6 weeks.
4. Strain and pour into a bottle. Keeps refrigerated for at least 6 months.

I usually finish my béarnaise sauce with a few drops of Worcestershire sauce, which gives the sauce additional character. Worcestershire sauce is also nice added to caramelised onion, barbecue sauce, and stews.

ENGLISH BROWN SAUCE

makes 500 ml (17 fl oz)

700 ml (24 fl oz) tomato passata (puréed tomatoes)
3 pitted dates
2½ tablespoons molasses
1 brown onion, chopped
1 lemon, sliced
2 tablespoons lemon juice
1 dried red chilli
1 teaspoon dark soy sauce
100 ml (3½ fl oz) malt vinegar
2½ tablespoons apple cider vinegar
1 tablespoon white vinegar
2 tablespoons tamarind purée
2½ tablespoons Worcestershire sauce
3 pieces mace
1 pinch ground cardamom
1 x 3 cm piece ginger, finely chopped
1 teaspoon black peppercorns
½ teaspoon allspice berries

1. Combine all ingredients in a saucepan and bring to the boil.
2. Reduce to a simmer and simmer for 1½ hours or until thickened.
3. Pass through a wide-mesh sieve or a metal colander to make a smooth sauce. Pour into a sterilised bottle.
4. Keeps refrigerated for about 6 months.

Every British pub offers HP Sauce along with mustard and ketchup. It has a tomatoey and slightly acidic flavour, and is indispensible in a full English breakfast. My version has a tart undertone, which contrasts nicely with the sweetness. If you want a sweeter sauce, add another date or some more molasses.

HOISIN SAUCE

makes 500 ml (17 fl oz)

2½ tablespoons light
  brown sugar
1 tablespoon molasses
1 tablespoon fermented
  black beans
1 garlic clove, crushed
2 tablespoons light soy
  sauce
3 tablespoons treacle
1 tablespoon sesame oil
1 tablespoon rice vinegar
1 pinch Five Spice (page 113)
1 teaspoon tahini
3–4 splashes of sriracha,
  (page 49)

1. Combine all ingredients and 3 tablespoons water in a saucepan. Bring to the boil, reduce to a simmer and simmer for 5–6 minutes. The sauce should thicken slightly, and will keep thickening once it's been blended and has cooled.
2. Remove saucepan from heat and cool slightly. Blend the sauce with a hand-held blender until smooth.
3. Pass through a sieve, pressing with the back of a spoon to extract as much sauce as possible.
4. Pour into a sterilised bottle or jar with tight-fitting lid and store in a cool, dark place.
5. Hoisin sauce will keep for at least 3 months, often longer. If you feel that the sauce is too thin when it's cooled you can boil it again to reduce it further.

TERIYAKI SAUCE

makes 300 ml (10½ fl oz)

200 ml (7 fl oz) light soy
  sauce
100 ml (3½ fl oz) mirin
100 ml (3½ fl oz) sake
2½ tablespoons light
  brown sugar

1. Combine all ingredients in a saucepan and simmer for 20 minutes or until thickened. Pour into a sterilised bottle with a tight-fitting lid.
2. Keeps refrigerated for at least 2 weeks.

PONZU SAUCE

makes 300 ml (10½ fl oz)

Dashi

1 strip kombu, 10 x 3 cm
  (inches in brackets)
15 g (½ oz) bonito flakes

Ponzu

2½ tablespoons rice vinegar
2½ tablespoons light soy
  sauce
2 tablespoons mirin
100 ml (3½ fl oz) dashi
2½ tablespoons yuzu juice

1. Combine 500 ml (2 cups) water and kombu in a saucepan and slowly bring to the boil, removing kombu right before water starts to boil. Remove from heat, add bonito flakes and steep for 10 minutes. Strain through a fine sieve. Dashi will keep refrigerated in an airtight container for 3–5 days, extra can be used in soups.
2. Combine all ingredients for ponzu, except yuzu juice, in a saucepan. Bring to the boil, reduce to a simmer, and simmer for a few minutes. Cool, then add the yuzu juice.
3. Pour into a sterilised bottle and refrigerate for 2 days before serving. Keeps refrigerated for about 1 month.

> If you're unable to find yuzu juice you may replace it by combining lime juice, orange juice, and grapefruit juice. I like serving ponzu as an accompaniment for raw and semi–raw foods such as sashimi and tataki, and crisp tempura vegetables.

AMERICAN BARBECUE SAUCE

makes 300 ml (10½ fl oz)

2½ tablespoons maple syrup
300 ml (10½ fl oz) tomato sauce (ketchup)
1 tablespoon lemon juice
1 tablespoon apple cider vinegar
2½ tablespoons light brown sugar
1 tablespoon smoked paprika
½ teaspoon garlic powder
1 teaspoon onion powder
1 splash of Tabasco

1. Combine all ingredients, 1 teaspoon salt and 1 pinch freshly ground black pepper in a saucepan. Bring to the boil, reduce heat to low, and simmer for 30 minutes or until thickened and reduced.
2. Pour the warm sauce into sterilised bottles with tight-fitting lids.
3. Sauce keeps refrigerated for about 1 month.

> Every self-respecting American barbecue joint makes their own sauce. This version is pretty sweet, with a bright tomato flavour and a bit of smokiness. If you want it to be even smokier, add a chipotle chilli while it boils.

SSAM BARBECUE SAUCE

makes 200 ml (7 fl oz)

1 tablespoon gochujang
1 tablespoon doenjang
1 teaspoon gochugaru
2 tablespoons tomato paste (concentrated purée)
55 g (2 oz) apple sauce
1 tablespoon white sugar
1 tablespoon sherry vinegar
1 tablespoon sesame oil
1 teaspoon confit garlic paste (page 120)
1 tablespoon light soy sauce
½ teaspoon onion powder
1 tablespoon white miso paste

1. Combine all ingredients, except miso, in a saucepan with 2½ tablespoons water and whisk until smooth. Bring to the boil, reduce heat and simmer for 3–4 minutes or until slightly thickened.
2. Add miso, stirring until sauce is smooth.
3. Pour into a sterilised glass bottle with a tight-fitting lid and refrigerate until needed. Keeps refrigerated for about 3 months.

> This sauce is inspired by David Chang's Momofuko SSÄM Sauce, a staple at all his restaurants since 2004. Chang likes to say that his sauce goes with every kind of food, from pizza to fried rice, and I agree. Gochujang, doenjang and gochugaru are available from Korean and Asian grocers.

BULGOGI BARBECUE SAUCE

makes 300 ml (10½ fl oz)

200 ml (7 fl oz) light soy sauce
3 tablespoons white sugar .
1 tablespoon sesame oil
2 tablespoons mirin
4 garlic cloves, finely grated
2 puréed pears
4 French shallots, finely chopped
1 tablespoon toasted sesame seeds

1. Combine soy sauce, sugar, oil, mirin, garlic and half of the pear purée in a saucepan, bring to the boil and boil for 5 minutes or until thickened. Cool, then refrigerate. Keeps refrigerated for up to 1 week.
2. When ready to use, combine the remaining puréed pear, shallots, and sesame seeds with the sauce and add it to the meat you want to marinate. Refrigerate to marinate for at least 30 minutes, ideally overnight.

> Grill sliced pork or a nicely marbled chuck steak after marinating in the bulgogi sauce. Now you can die happy.

SALSA LIZANO

makes 400 ml (14 fl oz)

1 dried guajillo chilli,
  stem removed, halved,
  seeds removed
1 brown onion, chopped
1 carrot, grated
1 tablespoon canola oil
1 tablespoon onion powder
1 teaspoon mustard powder
1 tablespoon ground cumin
½ teaspoon garlic powder
1 teaspoon ground turmeric
2 tablespoons white sugar
1 tablespoon white wine
  vinegar
1 tablespoon molasses
1 tablespoon tamarind purée

1. Toast chilli in a hot, dry frying pan for 30 seconds each side or until fragrant. Add 200 ml (7 fl oz) water and boil for 2–3 minutes. Pour mixture into bowl and set aside.
2. Sauté onion and carrot in oil until they soften, but don't let them colour. Transfer to a bowl and set aside.
3. Toast dry spices, sugar and ½ teaspoon freshly ground black pepper in a dry frying pan for a few minutes. Add chilli mix and simmer for a minute or so.
4. Blend chilli and spice mix with carrot, onion, 1 teaspoon salt and remaining ingredients in a blender until a smooth sauce. Add 1 tablespoon water if it seems too thick. Pour into sterilised glass bottles with tight-fitting lids.
5. Salsa Lizano will keep refrigerated for at least 1 month. It's nice with black beans, rice, fried fish, or quesadillas.

> I discovered this sauce a few years ago when I spent a few months in Costa Rica. Salsa Lizano, also known as Salsa inglese since it's reminiscent of HP sauce, can be found on every Costa Rican dining table, served with most foods.

PEBRE

makes 400 ml (14 fl oz)

1 brown onion, finely
  chopped
2 tomatoes, finely chopped
½ green capsicum, finely
  chopped
2 garlic cloves, finely
  chopped
½ long red chilli, finely
  chopped
20 g (²/₃ cup) finely
  chopped coriander
  (cilantro)
2½ tablespoons finely
  chopped oregano
2 tablespoons lemon juice
2 tablespoons white wine
  vinegar
1 tablespoon olive oil

1. Combine all ingredients in a bowl and season to taste.
2. Transfer to a glass jar. Pebre will keeps refrigerated for 3–4 days.

> Pebre hails from Chile, where it's served with most meals. It's easy to make and delicious with grilled meat and fish.

PLUM SAUCE

makes 1 litre (35 fl oz)

1 kg (2 lb 4 oz) plums
100 ml (3½ fl oz) apple
  cider vinegar
90 g (3¼ oz) light brown
  sugar
2½ tablespoons light soy
  sauce
2 garlic cloves
1 x 4 cm piece ginger, grated
1 star anise

1. Cut the plums into quarters and discard stones.
2. Combine all ingredients in a saucepan. Bring to boil and boil for 20–25 minutes until plums are thoroughly soft.
3. Cool slightly, then blend the sauce in a blender until smooth. Pass through a fine sieve and pour into sterilised bottles with tight-fitting lids.
4. Keeps refrigerated for about 1 month.

> This sauce is nice with Chinese food—it's excellent as a dip for fried spring rolls, or served with pork or crispy duck. Or perhaps with foie gras, where it offers a nice contrast to the richness of the liver. It can be made with most types of plums—when your local plums are in season, they'll be the most delicious.

OYSTER SAUCE

makes 300 ml (10½ fl oz)

6 oysters, shucked
2½ white sugar
2 tablespoons light
  brown sugar
100 ml (3½ fl oz) light soy
  sauce
1 teaspoon dark soy sauce
100 ml (3½ fl oz) mirin

1. Add oysters and their juices to a saucepan. Add 300 ml (10½ fl oz) water and bring to boil. Reduce heat to low and simmer, covered, for about 10 minutes or until thickened.
2. Remove from heat, add 1 teaspoon salt, and blend to a smooth sauce. Pour into a container and cool. Cover with a lid or plastic wrap and refrigerate for 1 day to infuse.
3. Strain the oyster water through a sieve, pressing with the back of a spoon to extract as much liquid as possible.
4. Place sugars in a saucepan and heat over medium heat without stirring until the sugar begins to caramelise. It should have the colour of light treacle. Carefully add oyster water, light and dark soy sauce and mirin. Simmer for 10 minutes or until reduced by about one-third.
5. Pour sauce into a sterilised glass bottle or jar with a tight-fitting lid.
6. Keeps refrigerated for at least 1 month. Oyster sauce is especially good with steamed vegetables like Chinese broccoli, watercress, or broccolini—perhaps topped with toasted sesame seeds.

STEAMED BROCCOLINI WITH OYSTER SAUCE AND FRIED SHALLOTS

Serves 4 people

400 g (14 oz) broccolini
100 ml (3½ fl oz) oyster
  sauce (page 62)

Fried shallots

200 g (7 oz) small red Asian
  shallots, thinly sliced
Peanut oil, for deep-frying

1. Heat oil in a heavy-based saucepan to 170°C (325°F; a cube of bread will turn golden in 20 seconds).
2. Fry shallots for a few minutes until crisp and golden brown. Drain on paper towel.
3. Put broccolini in a metal or bamboo steamer. Cover with a tight-fitting lid and steam over a saucepan or wok of simmering water for 3–4 minutes, or until just cooked through.
4. Arrange broccolini on serving platter, pour oyster sauce over it and top with fried shallots. Serve immediately.

> This is a perfect side for meat and chicken. Quick, tasty, and healthy. This cooking method suits most green vegetables, such as broccoli, morning glory, and spinach.

CHIMICHURRI

makes 200 ml (7 fl oz)

*½ dried guajillo chilli, halved,
stem and seeds removed*
2 garlic cloves
*15 g (¼ cup) finely chopped
flat-leaf parsley*
*2½ tablespoons finely
chopped oregano*
1 tablespoon dried oregano
150 ml (5 fl oz) olive oil
*1½ tablespoons red wine
vinegar*

1. Toast chilli in a hot, dry frying pan for 2–3 minutes until fragrant. Finely grind chilli with a mortar and pestle, or cut into small pieces with a sharp knife.
2. Add chilli to a bowl with remaining ingredients, ½ teaspoon salt and ½ teaspoon freshly ground black pepper, stir to combine, then transfer to a sterilised glass jar with a tight-fitting lid. Keeps for at least 1 month.

> Argentinians often keep chimichurri at room temperature, and many feel it tastes better the longer it sits. As long as the chimichurri doesn't start to go mouldy you can go ahead and serve it with your piece of grilled meat. Or store it in the fridge instead—it's up to you.

TACO SALSA

makes 400 ml (14 fl oz)

*400 g (14 oz) canned whole
tomatoes*
*1 green jalapeño, coarsely
chopped*
*1 brown onion, coarsely
chopped*
*1 tablespoon Mexican hot
sauce (page 43)*
*1 tablespoon apple cider
vinegar*

1. Blend all ingredients in a food processor to a smooth sauce but still with some texture.
2. Season to taste and pour into sterilised jars.
3. Keeps refrigerated for at least 1 week.

> The heat in the salsa is regulated by the amount of hot sauce. Make a milder salsa by either removing the jalapeño seeds, or swapping it for green capsicum.

MUSHROOM SOY SAUCE

makes 500 ml (17 fl oz)

*750 g (1 lb 10 oz)
mushrooms (button or
whatever's available)*
3 tablespoons fine sea salt
*350 ml (12 fl oz) red wine
vinegar*

1. Cut mushrooms into quarters and place in a large bowl. Sprinkle with salt and cover with a lid. Leave in a cool, dark place for 5 days. Stir once a day and remove any mould.
2. Transfer mushrooms to a large saucepan. Add vinegar and bring to the boil. Reduce heat to low and simmer, uncovered, for 2 hours.
3. Pass liquid through muslin (cheesecloth). Discard solids.
4. Return to saucepan, bring to the boil, then pour the hot 'soy' into sterilised bottles with tight-fitting lids.
5. Store in a cool, dark place. Keeps for about 6 months. It can be used to give a jolt of umami to stews and sauces.

VINEGARS

We get vinegar when wine, or some other alcoholic liquid, oxidises in a process that turns ethanol into acetic acid. You can make vinegar from most alcoholic drinks as long as the alcohol level isn't too high—too much alcohol can kill the bacteria in the vinegar mother, and without the mother there's no vinegar. So various types of wine, cider, Champagne, and beer are perfect for making vinegar. If you're lucky, time and acidity will make wine turn into vinegar of its own accord, but I recommend using either a so-called 'mother of vinegar', or an unfiltered and unpasteurised vinegar as a starter. This method speeds up and controls the process. You can find special glass and ceramic vinegar urns with taps at the base that allow you to harvest the mature vinegar little by little while the mother keeps floating up top. Such tools are clever, but I find that a large glass jar with lid works just as well. It doesn't let you produce the same amount of vinegar, and it's a bit more complicated to siphon it off, but jars take up less space than urns and you probably already have a few at home.

MOTHER OF VINEGAR

The mother of vinegar is a type of starter containing the bacteria required to turn alcohol into acetic acid. A mother of vinegar is pretty unappetising —a rubbery collection of bacteria that resembles Slime from the '90s. You could be fortunate enough to find a spontaneously fermented mother in a forgotten bottle of vinegar at the back of your pantry. Or perhaps you have a vinegar-making friend who can give you a piece of their mother. If all else fails, you can order one online.

It's also pretty straightforward to cultivate your own mother of vinegar from scratch. The quickest process uses apple cider or red wine vinegar, which should ideally be organic, unfiltered, and unpasteurised. These tend to contain a live bacterial culture and can usually be found in health food stores or organic grocers. Try unscrewing the cork to let fresh air in, and with a bit of luck you'll have a mother of vinegar in a few weeks. Increase your chances by making sure the bottle isn't entirely full, and by storing it at room temperature. Another, and in my experience, a slightly quicker method, involves half-filling a glass jar with vinegar, adding a bit of wine, and covering the whole thing with muslin (cheesecloth). A few weeks later you should find a gelatinous disk floating on top: that's the mother of vinegar. It will be thin in the beginning, but soon grows more robust. Once it's 2–3 millimetres thick it's ready to use.

As noted it is possible to make vinegar without a mother. If this is your chosen method, I strongly recommend using an unfiltered and unpasteurised vinegar as the starter. A mother will usually form during the production process—it just takes a bit longer.

TIPS FOR VINEGAR SUCCESS

My vinegar experiments have led me to conclude that apple cider, red wine, and malt vinegars are both easiest and quickest. They make for good beginner vinegars, gateways to an exciting world of possibilities.

Writing vinegar recipes is difficult since so much of it is about feeling it out, and to some extent about luck. But here are a few important principles for success in vinegar making:

Alcohol content

Vinegar can be made from most liquids that either contain alcohol or produce it in the fermentation process. But in order for the acetic acid bacteria to thrive, the alcohol content of your vinegar base should be about 7–12%. A wine with a higher alcohol content can easily be diluted with water.

Temperature

I recommend room temperature—around 18–22°C (65–72°F)—for the acetic acid bacteria to thrive. If it's too cold, the transformation into vinegar will either be very slow or won't happen at all. You can make vinegar in conditions of up to 25°C (77°F), but at higher temperatures the bacteria risk growing too quickly. What's more, at higher temperatures the wine can evaporate before it's become vinegar.

Oxygen

The bacteria required to make vinegar need oxygen to live, so don't cover your vinegar vessel with a lid, though you can use muslin (cheesecloth) or a piece of fabric to keep dust and fruit flies at bay. It's advantageous to use a large, wide-mouthed jar or urn to expose as much wine to the air as possible. It's also best not to fill your vessel all the way up—about halfway, or two-thirds, should be enough. I use glass jars that hold about 4 litres (about 1 gallon).

Tools

Avoid metal tools and containers in vinegar making. Metal is said to affect the taste and even react with the bacteria. (I, however, have not experienced this as a major problem.)

Do not disturb

The mother is sensitive and does not like travelling or being moved. Disturbances can cause her to sink, and she's difficult to lure back to the surface. Leave the mother alone, refrain from stirring or generally fiddling with her.

High-quality ingredients

The taste of the base ingredient determines the taste of your vinegar, and a high-quality base product yields a high-quality final product. Bad wine, for example corked wine, doesn't provide the requisite conditions. Wine rich in sulphites isn't particularly suitable for vinegar-making either as they can kill the mother. Sulphites are the most common additives in wine, but they also occur naturally at various levels depending on the grape, year, fermentation method, and type of barrel used. There are generally more sulphites in white than in red wine, and sweeter types of wine have more than dry. Sulphite levels tend to decrease as wine is aged, such that the older the wine, the lower the sulphite level. Boxed wines often contain high levels of sulphite, which makes them unsuitable for vinegar making. Natural wines have no or minimal sulphite additives, making them excellent vinegar bases.

Multiple batches

It's a good idea to have several batches going at once when you're making vinegar. Keep one urn for making luxury vinegar from one single type of high-quality wine, and one for a simpler type of cooking vinegar, where you continuously add wine you didn't finish drinking and siphon off vinegar.

Birds of a feather?

It's possible to use a mother made from a different type of liquid than the one you're turning into vinegar. But in my experience the result in terms of both colour and flavour is better when you use an apple cider mother to make apple cider vinegar, a red wine mother for a red wine vinegar, and so forth.

VINEGAR

1. Crema di balsamico
2. Elderflower vinegar
3. White wine vinegar
4. Malt vinegar
5. Shallot vinegar
6. Raspberry vinegar
7. Red wine vinegar
8. Apple cider vinegar
9. Tarragon vinegar

BASIC VINEGAR RECIPE

2 parts vinegar base, such as wine, cider, beer, or some other alcoholic drink, diluted to about 7–12% alcohol if necessary

1 part vinegar with mother, or unfiltered and unpasteurised vinegar

1. Clean a large glass jar with a removable lid that's big enough to hold double the total volume of liquid.

2. Pour vinegar base into the jar, then add vinegar, and stir with a teaspoon. If you are using a mother, cautiously place it in the jar at the very end, making sure it floats on top. Don't worry if it sinks at first, it's very likely that it will float up, but you still want to give your vinegar the best conditions.

3. Cover the jar with a piece of fabric, muslin (cheesecloth), or similar. Secure with a rubber band.

4. Store the jar somewhere dark if possible, or at least out of direct sunlight. It should be around 18–22°C (65-72°F).

5. Check on the jar every now and then. A mother of vinegar usually forms after 1–3 weeks. It will keep growing thicker, a sign that you're on track. If you find mould instead, it is likely that the jar is stored somewhere too hot, or the liquid might have come into contact with other bacteria, perhaps from a hand. This unfortunately means you'll have to throw it out and start over. Don't worry if the mother of vinegar sinks—it only means she's full. A new mother will usually form after a while. But you can also feed the mother some more wine to make a larger batch of vinegar. The added wine will return her to the surface.

6. After 5 weeks or so, depending on what type of vinegar you're making, you can start checking to see if it's ready. You'll know it's almost there when the smell is sour and makes your nose sting. From then on, your taste and preference will determine when it's done.

7. Once you're happy with the taste, remove the mother together with about 100 ml (31/2 fl oz) of vinegar, and use it to make a new batch.

8. Strain the rest of the vinegar through a few layers of coffee filters to make a clear vinegar. If using a "living vinegar" makes you uncomfortable, you can kill the bacteria by carefully heating it to and holding it at 50°C (120°F) and for about 10 minutes.

9. Pour into sterilised bottles. The vinegar is now ready to use, though ageing it for an additional month or so helps the flavours fully develop.

APPLE CIDER VINEGAR

2 parts high-quality dry apple cider (ideally organic), or an unfiltered apple juice
1 part unfiltered (ideally unpasteurised) apple cider vinegar, preferably with the mother

1. Follow the basic recipe.
2. With apple cider the entire process from cider to vinegar will take about 6–8 weeks.

> It's possible to make vinegar from apple juice even though it doesn't contain any alcohol. Alcohol is often produced during the fermentation process, subsequently turning into vinegar.

WHITE WINE VINEGAR AND CHAMPAGNE VINEGAR

2 parts dry or semi-dry white wine, Champagne, or sparkling wine (ideally organic and sulphite-free)
1 part unfiltered (ideally unpasteurised) white wine vinegar, preferably with the mother

1. Follow the basic recipe.
2. With white wine and Champagne vinegar the full process takes at least 3 months.

> The method for making white wine and Champagne vinegar follows that of making other types of vinegars, only requiring more time. These types of vinegars tend to be more difficult than others. A few recommendations for making your own white wine vinegar:
>
> • Use a dry or semi-dry wine, since vinegar should have a fresh acidity.
> • Ideally use a wine free from sulphites, a so-called natural wine. Other wines may still work, but too much sulphite will kill the mother. White cask wines, for example, are high in sulphites and are not suitable for vinegar making.

OYSTERS WITH SHALLOT VINAIGRETTE

serves 4 people

12 oysters
2 tablespoons finely
* chopped shallots*
100 ml (3½ fl oz) red wine
* vinegar*

1. Combine shallot and vinegar in a bowl.
2. To open oysters, hold oyster by the rounded end with a tea towel, flat-side up. Insert tip of an oyster knife into hinged end of oyster, prying it open. Separate the muscle from the meat by running the knife along the shell. Remove top shell. Arrange oysters on a bed of ice, and serve with the vinaigrette.

RED WINE VINEGAR

2 parts red wine
1 part unfiltered (ideally
* unpasteurised) red wine*
* vinegar, preferably with*
* the mother*

1. Follow the basic vinegar recipe (page 76).
2. Red wine vinegar takes about 2 months to ferment.

MALT VINEGAR

2 parts beer
1 part unfiltered (ideally
* unpasteurised) apple*
* cider vinegar, preferably*
* with the mother*

1. Follow the basic vinegar recipe (page 76).
2. It takes about 6–8 weeks for the beer to turn into vinegar.

> I find malt vinegar quite easy to make—it's a good beginner's vinegar. Malt vinegar is popular in England, and an essential ingredient in fish and chips. Try swapping apple cider vinegar for malt vinegar in sauces for a different character.

INFUSED VINEGAR

SHALLOT
For 500 ml (17 fl oz)

*500 ml (17 fl oz) white wine
vinegar
6 shallots, quartered*

1. Place shallot in a sterilised glass jar.
2. Add vinegar and leave at room temperature for 5–7 days.
3. Pass through a sieve and pour into a sterilised bottle.
   Keeps essentially forever.

TARRAGON
For 500 ml (17 fl oz)

*500 ml (17 fl oz) white wine
vinegar
8 tarragon sprigs*

1. Rinse tarragon and place in a sterilised glass jar.
2. Add vinegar and leave at room temperature for 5–7 days.
3. Pass through a sieve and pour into a sterilised bottle.
   Keeps essentially forever.

ELDERFLOWER
For 500 ml (17 fl oz)

*500 ml (17 fl oz) white wine
vinegar
5 bunches elderflower*

1. Place elderflower in a sterilised glass jar.
2. Add vinegar and leave at room temperature for 5–7 days.
3. Pass through a sieve and pour into a sterilised bottle.
   Keeps essentially forever.

RASPBERRY
For 500 ml (17 fl oz)

*500 ml (17 fl oz) red wine
vinegar
100 g (3½ oz) raspberries*

1. Place raspberries in a sterilised glass jar.
2. Add vinegar and leave at room temperature for 5–7 days.
3. Pass through a sieve and pour into a sterilised bottle.
   Keeps essentially forever.

CREMA DI BALSAMICO

For 150 ml

*300 ml balsamic vinegar
100 ml brown sugar
35 g (1¼ oz) raisins*

1. Combine all ingredients in a saucepan and bring to
   the boil. Reduce heat and simmer until only 200 ml
   (7 fl oz) remains, about 15 minutes.
2. Transfer to a blender, blend until smooth and pass
   through a sieve.
3. Pour into a sterilised bottle. Keeps refrigerated for
   many months.

Shallot vinegar, tarragon vinegar and
raspberry vinegar.

PICKLES AND PRESERVES

In the past people canned and pickled their foods to extend the bounty of the seasons. These days we can get fresh produce year round, but I'm still fond of canning fruit and vegetables while they're in peak season to better enjoy them during the rest of the year.

Then there's the fact that pickling adds another dimension of flavour, a nice acidity that goes particularly well with smoked fish, pork, pâté and other fatty foods.

In the Nordic countries the most common pickling principle is 1–2–3: that is, one part white vinegar, two parts sugar, and three parts water. But you can easily swap white vinegar for other types of vinegar, and water for a different liquid to add flavour and variation—try soy sauce or beer.

For hard root vegetables and larger vegetable pieces, you should ideally use a warm pickling liquid. Not only does this make them softer, but it also opens up the cells, allowing better absorption of the liquid. Soft vegetables, however, should be pickled raw and in cold pickling liquid. For an extra kick, you can add spices to the liquid. Mustard seeds and coriander seeds are a great place to start.

Pickles should be stored cold, ideally in the refrigerator. And be careful not to stick your fingers into the jar as that's a sure-fire way of shortening the shelf life. If you take care to store your pickles properly, they'll keep for a long time. That said, I find that over time the vinegar can dilute the flavour of the vegetables themselves, how fast that happens depends on what you've pickled—pickled onion is best in the first two or three days after pickling, while gari keeps for months.

PICKLES AND PRESERVES

1. Preserved tarragon
2. Pickled mustard seeds
3. Pickled onion
4. Preserved lemons
5. Mango chutney
6. Gari
7. Antipasto pickles
8. Soy-sauce pickled mushrooms
9. Vietnamese pickles
10. Pickled jalapeño

PICKLED JALAPEÑO

You'll need a 500 ml (17 fl oz) jar

200 g jalapeños, quartered

Pickling liquid

2½ tablespoons white sugar
2½ tablespoons white vinegar
2½ tablespoons apple cider vinegar
½ teaspoon coriander seeds
½ teaspoon black peppercorns

1. For pickling liquid, combine all ingredients with 150 ml (5 fl oz) water in a saucepan and bring to the boil. Remove from heat and leave to cool.
2. Place quartered jalapeño in a sterilised glass jar with a tight-fitting lid.
3. Fill with the cold pickling liquid and let sit for a few hours before serving.
4. Keeps refrigerated for 2–3 weeks.

PICKLED ONION

You'll need a 500 ml (17 fl oz) jar

4 red onions, thinly sliced

Pickling liquid

2½ tablespoons white vinegar
125 g (4½ oz) white sugar
Pinch of crushed black peppercorns

1. For pickling liquid, combine vinegar, sugar and 300 ml (10½ fl oz) water in a saucepan, bring to the boil and cook until sugar has dissolved. Remove from heat and leave to cool.
2. Place onion in a glass jar with a tight-fitting lid and add pickling liquid.
3. Let sit for at least 1 hour before serving. Pickled onion keeps refrigerated for about 1 week.

PRESERVED TARRAGON

You'll need a 100 ml (3½ fl oz) jar

2 tablespoons white wine vinegar
1 handful tarragon leaves

1. Combine vinegar and 1 tablespoon water.
2. Stuff tarragon leaves into a sterilised glass jar with a tight-fitting lid that holds about 100 ml (3½ fl oz).
3. Add vinegar mixture to cover.
4. Store in a cool place. Keeps for about 6 months.

> If you grow tarragon in the summer and preserve the leaves you'll be able to enjoy béarnaise sauce throughout the winter months.

The peels are the main attraction here, but feel free to include the juice as well. Preserved lemons work well in most situations where regular lemon might be used, but it's extra successful in Moroccan food, cold sauce, or served with chicken.

PRESERVED LEMONS

You'll need a 1 litre (35 fl oz) jar

1 kg (2 lb 4 oz) organic lemons
50 g (1¾ oz) sea salt flakes

1. Thoroughly wash and scrub lemons.
2. Cut lemons in half. Juice 4–5 of the lemons to get about 100 ml (3½ fl oz) juice. Transfer juice to a bowl along with the remaining lemon halves. Add salt and toss to coat.
3. Stuff lemon halves and salt into a sterilised glass jar with a tight-fitting lid until the jar is completely full. Add juice, followed by enough water to cover lemons.
4. Leave in a cool, dark place for 4 weeks.
5. Lemons will keep for 6 months and should be kept in the fridge once the jar has been opened.

PICKLED CHERRIES

You'll need two 500 ml (17 fl oz) jar

600 g (4 cups) cherries

Pickling liquid

100 ml (3½ fl oz) sherry vinegar
175 g (6 oz) white sugar
4 star anise

1. Remove pits from cherries and divide cherries between glass jars with tight-fitting lids.
2. Combine vinegar, sugar, star anise and 400 ml (14 fl oz) water in a saucepan, bring to the boil and boil until sugar has dissolved.
3. Pour the hot liquid over cherries and seal lids. Let sit for an hour or so before serving.
4. Keeps for about a month. Once opened, store in the fridge. Pickled cherries go especially well with rich foods like duck, paté, or Iberian ham.

VIETNAMESE PICKLES

You'll need a 1 litre (35 fl oz) jar

150 g (5½ oz) carrot, cut into matchsticks
150 g (5½ oz) daikon, cut into matchsticks
100 g (3½ oz) radishes, thinly sliced

Pickling liquid

2 tablespoons white sugar
100 ml (3½ fl oz) rice vinegar
1 teaspoon coriander seeds
½ teaspoon cumin seeds

1. For pickling liquid, combine all ingredients with 150 ml (5 fl oz) water in a saucepan, bring to the boil and boil until sugar has dissolved. Remove from heat and cool.
2. Fill a jar with a tight-fitting lid with vegetables and add pickling liquid.
3. Let sit for a few hours before serving.
4. Keeps refrigerated for 2–3 weeks.

> These pickles can have a strong smell, but don't worry—it's only the particular scent of daikon. If you find it unpleasant you can always leave it out.

Preserved lemons   PICKLES AND PRESERVES **89**

GRILLED MACKEREL WITH PICKLED GREEN TOMATOES AND CRESS

serves 4 people
*4 whole mackerel, deboned
  with tails left on*
2½ tablespoons olive oil

For serving
*Cress and pickled green
  tomatoes*

1. Heat a char-grill pan to medium–high heat. Brush the mackerel with oil and grill for 4–5 minutes each side or until meat easily comes away from the bone. Season to taste.
2. Transfer to plates and drizzle with olive oil. Serve topped with cress and pickled tomatoes.

PICKLED GREEN TOMATOES

You'll need two 700 ml (24 fl oz) jars
*1 kg (2 lb 4 oz) green
  tomatoes*

Pickling liquid
*100 ml (3½ fl oz) white
  vinegar*
175 g (6 oz) white sugar

1. For pickling liquid, combine vinegar, sugar and 300 ml (10½ fl oz) water in a saucepan, bring to the boil and boil until sugar has dissolved. Remove from heat and cool completely.
2. Cut tomatoes into large dice and place in glass jars with tight-fitting lids. Add pickling liquid and seal jars.
3. Keeps refrigerated for 2–3 weeks.

> Green tomatoes are well-suited for pickling since their flesh is fairly hard with an invigorating acidity. Never heard of green tomatoes? They're just regular unripe tomatoes, but they can be a bit tricky to find in stores. During the summer you should be able to get them in well-stocked grocers, or you might grow them yourself. Pickled, they taste good with grilled fish and in salads.

PICKLED MUSTARD SEEDS

**You'll need a 300 ml
(10½ fl oz) jar**
*70 g (2½ oz) yellow
    mustard seeds*

Pickling liquid
*2½ tablespoons rice vinegar
2 tablespoons white sugar*

1. For pickling liquid, combine vinegar, sugar, 55 ml
   (1¾ fl oz) water and ½ tablespoon salt in a saucepan,
   bring to the boil, and boil until sugar has dissolved.
   Remove from heat and cool.
2. Bring a saucepan of water to the boil and add mustard
   seeds. Boil for 1 minute, then discard water and rinse
   mustard seeds with cold water. Repeat the boiling and
   rinsing process, then drain mustard seeds in a sieve.
3. Transfer seeds to a sterilised glass jar with a tight-fitting
   lid and add pickling liquid. Let sit for at least 3 hours.
4. Pickled mustard seeds will keep refrigerated for about
   1 month.

> Nice with steak tartare, or as a substitute for mustard.

SOY-SAUCE PICKLED MUSHROOMS

**You'll need a 700 ml
(24 fl oz) jar**
*2 teaspoons canola oil
600 g (1 lb 5 oz)
    mushrooms, such
    as oyster or shiitake
    mushrooms*

Pickling liquid
*2½ tablespoons rice vinegar
2½ tablespoons white sugar
200 ml (7 fl oz) light soy
    sauce*

1. Heat oil in a very hot frying pan, add mushrooms and
   sauté quickly until golden. Season to taste. Transfer
   mushrooms to a sterilised glass jar with tight-fitting lid.
2. For pickling liquid, combine vinegar, sugar, soy sauce and
   200 ml (7 fl oz) water in a saucepan, bring to the boil
   and boil until sugar has dissolves. Add pickling liquid
   to the mushrooms and seal lid.
3. Keeps refrigerated for 2–3 weeks.

> The friendship between mushrooms and soy sauce is famous.
> I like serving the soy sauce pickled mushroom with rice
> courses, in sandwiches, and in ramen.

PICKLED MUSHROOMS

You'll need a 1 litre (35 fl oz) jar

300 g (10½ oz) fresh chanterelle, yellow foot, or similar mushrooms (or the same amount of dried and soaked mushrooms)

Pickling liquid

100 ml (3½ fl oz) white vinegar
350 g (12 oz) white sugar
1 teaspoon black peppercorns
2 dried bay leaves
1 x 3 cm (1¼ in) piece ginger, finely grated
2 teaspoons yellow mustard seeds
5 cloves
1 star anise

1. For pickling liquid, combine all ingredients with 500 ml (2 cups) water and 1 teaspoon salt.
2. In a large saucepan, bring to the boil, and boil until sugar has dissolved.
3. Clean mushrooms and add to the boiling liquid.
4. Reduce heat and simmer, stirring occasionally for about 1 hour.
5. Pour into a sterilised glass jar with a tight-fitting lid.
6. Store in a cool place. Keeps for months.

> These pickled mushrooms are sweet with a bit of heat from the ginger and mustard seeds. A perfect accompaniment to game or steak tartare.

GARI

You'll need a 500 ml (17 fl oz) jar

300 g (10½ oz) ginger, peeled and thinly sliced with a mandoline
2 teaspoons white sugar

Pickling liquid

100 ml (3½ fl oz) rice vinegar
2½ tablespoons white sugar

1. Combine ginger, sugar, and 2 teaspoons salt in a bowl and leave to marinate for about 20 minutes.
2. Meanwhile, for pickling liquid, combine vinegar, sugar and 55 ml (1¾ fl oz) water in a saucepan, bring to the boil and boil until sugar has dissolved. Remove from the heat and cool slightly.
3. Fill a saucepan with water and bring to the boil. Rinse ginger, then add to saucepan and boil it for about 1 minute. Discard water and rinse ginger in cold water. Squeeze out all liquid.
4. Place ginger in a sterilised jar with tight-fitting lid and add the pickling liquid. Let sit for at least 3 hours before serving.
5. Keeps refrigerated for a few months.

> You'll get the best results if you use young ginger, which can be recognised by the bright colour of the peel. You'll likely find it at Asian grocers. Gari is often served with sushi.

MANGO CHUTNEY

You'll need a 200 ml (7 fl oz) jar

Pinch of dried chilli flakes
½ teaspoon fennel seeds
½ teaspoon cumin seeds
½ teaspoon black cumin seeds
1 tablespoon canola oil
70 g (2½ oz) raw sugar
2 green (unripe) mangoes, peeled and cut into 2 cm (¾ in) dice

1. Toast spices in a hot, dry frying pan until fragrant. Coarsely grind with mortar and pestle.
3. Heat oil in a saucepan over medium–high heat, add all ingredients and 1 teaspoon salt and sauté, stirring occasionally, until sugar melts.
4. Add 100 ml (3½ fl oz) water, reduce to a simmer, and cook, stirring occasionally, for 20-25 minutes until mango is soft and looks translucent.
5. Transfer the warm chutney to a sterilised glass jar with a tight-fitting lid.
6. Keeps refrigerated for 6 months.

This chutney calls for green, unripe mango. Asian grocers often stock it, but if you can't find it, use a firm ripe mango. As long as it's not too soft and still fairly acidic it'll work here, otherwise you'll end up with a very sweet chutney that doesn't have the right texture.

ANTIPASTO PICKLES

You'll need a 2 litre (70 fl oz) jar

½ cauliflower, cut into florets
½ romanesco, cut into florets
1 long red chilli, coarsely chopped
1 fennel bulb, sliced
5 shallots, sliced

Pickling liquid

250 ml (1 cup) white wine vinegar
2½ tablespoons white sugar
2 teaspoons salt
½ teaspoon fennel seeds
½ teaspoon black peppercorns
½ teaspoon yellow mustard seeds
½ teaspoon coriander seeds
2 fresh bay leaves

1. For pickling liquid, combine all ingredients in a large saucepan with 500 ml (2 cups) water and 2 teaspoons salt. Bring to the boil, then remove from heat and cool.
2. Fill a sterilised glass jar with a tight-fitting lid with vegetables and add pickling liquid. Let sit for an hour or so before serving.
3. Keeps refrigerated for a few weeks after you've opened the jar.

> I like to serve these pickles with charcuterie. You can use all kinds of different vegetables for this recipe—carrot, capsicum and celery are excellent alternatives.

SPICE BLENDS

There are a few things to keep in mind when making dry spice blends. Use whole spices, and toast and grind them yourself. Spices should be stored in a dark and cool place; the common spot over the stove or in the window is not ideal. I tend to grind most of my spice blends in an electric coffee grinder as it's quick and offers an even grind, but if you prefer, you can use a mortar and pestle instead. In fact, for coarser blends I prefer a mortar and pestle, as the electric grinder can easily give you too fine of a grind.

It's fun to dry your own spices, vegetables, and herbs for these recipes. You can use a dehydrator specifically intended for the purpose, but a low oven works just as well. Or, if you can, hang them from your ceiling and let them dry at room temperature. Even the microwave works surprisingly well for drying herbs. Place them on paper towels and dry them in short bursts, making sure to keep an eye on them—I've set fire to my microwave while drying sage, and the neighbours were suspicious to say the least. Herbs well-suited for drying include bay leaf, thyme, rosemary, and sage. Leafy herbs like basil and coriander are better used fresh.

Whole spices keep for about a year, while ground spices and herbs keep their flavour for just a few months. So you can see that using a four-year old ground cumin in your recipes won't make anyone happy.

Wet spice blends and pastes should be stored in the fridge, where they usually have a long shelf life. They can also be frozen in small portions. Making your own spice pastes is not difficult, and the reward in terms of flavour is enormous. Green curry made with your own curry paste is worlds apart from one made with store-bought paste.

WET SPICE BLENDS

1. Chilli bean paste
2. Green curry paste
3. Tahini
4. Chipotle paste
5. Confit garlic paste
6. Harissa
7. Grilling oil
8. Truffle tapenade
9. Yellow curry paste

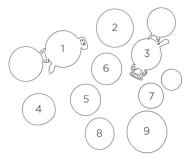

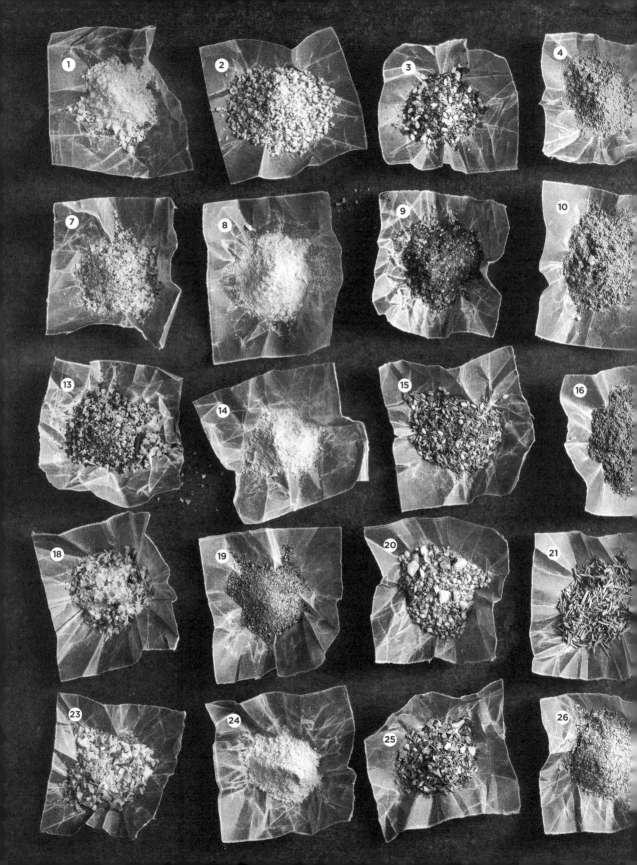

DRY SPICE BLENDS

1. Faux celery salt
2. Gomashio
3. Furikake
4. North Indian curry
5. Pork spice
6. Jerk spice
7. Celery salt
8. Leek powder
9. Barbecue rub
10. Garam masala
11. Salad spice
12. Taco spice
13. Ash salt
14. Onion powder
15. Za'atar
16. Five-spice
17. Fish spice
18. Sicilian spiced salt
19. Mushroom powder
20. Dukkah
21. Herbes de Provence
22. Chicken spice
23. Herb salt
24. Garlic powder
25. Persillade
26. Boullion powder
27. Leek ash

Dry spice blends keep for at least a year, but sometimes start losing their flavour after a few weeks. It's better to make smaller batches more often.

CHILLI BEAN PASTE

makes 200 ml (7 fl oz)
2½ tablespoons canola oil
200 g (7 oz) long red chillies,
 cored, seeds removed
 and finely chopped
50 g (1¾ oz) fermented
 black beans, rinsed and
 chopped
1 tablespoon white sugar
1 tablespoon chinkiang
 vinegar (black
 Chinese vinegar)

1. Heat oil in a frying pan over medium heat, add chilli and black beans and sauté, stirring occasionally, for 2–3 minutes until softened.
2. Add sugar and cook, stirring occasionally, for another 3 minutes or until dissolved. Stir in vinegar, then lower heat and simmer for another 5 minutes or until reduced.
3. Remove from heat and cool. Transfer to a sterilised glass jar with a tight-fitting lid. Keeps refrigerated for 1 month.

> Chilli bean paste is very popular in Chinese cooking, especially in the Sichuan kitchen. This variety is particularly suitable for stir fries. Try stir-frying pork belly strips with chilli bean paste. Add green onion toward the end and remove from heat when soft. Serve with rice, chilli oil, and Chinkiang vinegar. Chinkiang vinegar is available from Asian grocers.

CHIPOTLE PASTE

makes 200 ml (7 fl oz)
1 red capsicum (pepper)
4 long red chillies
2 dried chipotle chillies
1 dried ancho chilli
1 tablespoon olive oil
1 teaspoon white wine
 vinegar

1. Preheat the oven grill (broiler) to 230°C (450°F).
2. Grill (broil) capsicum and fresh chilli for about 15 minutes until they're completely black. Transfer to a bowl and cover tightly with plastic wrap for about 15 minutes.
3. Meanwhile, soak dried chilli in hot water for 20 minutes.
4. Discard seeds and remove the black peel from grilled chilli and capsicum.
5. Remove seeds from soaked chilli.
6. Roughly chop capsicum and grilled and soaked chillies. Add to a blender with oil and vinegar and blend to a paste. Add salt to taste.
7. Transfer to sterilised glass jar with a tight-fitting lid. Keeps refrigerated for about 2 months. Nice in marinades and recipes that require a soft, round heat with a bit of smokiness.

> For a delicious taco meat, rub chuck steak with chipotle paste and slow-grill over indirect heat, taking your time with it, until tender. Or combine the paste with mayonnaise for a chipotle mayo to serve with grilled corn cobs.

Harissa, confit garlic paste, yellow curry paste,
green curry paste, chilli bean paste, and chipotle paste.

HARISSA

makes 100 ml (3½ fl oz)

*150 g (5½ oz) long red
  chillies, seeds removed
2 garlic cloves with peel
½ teaspoon caraway seeds
½ teaspoon coriander seeds
½ teaspoon cumin seeds
20 g (¾ oz) dried aleppo
  chilli
1 tablespoon olive oil*

1. Preheat oven to 150°C (300°F).
2. Place chilli and garlic on a baking tray in centre of oven and roast for 20 minutes until dark. Peel garlic, then roughly chop garlic and chilli.
3. Toast dry spices in a dry frying pan until fragrant, then finely grind in a spice grinder.
4. Halve the dried chilli and remove seeds and stem. Toast in a hot, dry frying pan for 2–3 minutes each side until fragrant.
5. Bring a saucepan of water to a boil and remove from heat. Add dried chilli and leave to soak for 15-20 minutes.
6. Save a few tablespoons of chilli water and discard the rest. Roughly chop the chilli.
7. Blend all ingredients and ½ teaspoon salt with a hand-held blender to a smooth paste. If the harissa feels too thick or is difficult to blend you can add 2-3 tablespoons reserved chilli water. Add more salt to taste if desired.
8. Transfer to a glass jar with tight-fitting lid. Keeps refrigerated for about 1 month.

> There are innumerable varieties of harissa, so take this as your chance to adapt the recipe according to your own taste. For a stronger sauce, use a hotter type of chilli. For a milder variety, swap out half of the fresh chilli for the same amount of capsicum. A bit of lemon juice or dried mint is yet another way to give the harissa a different character.

TAHINI

makes 200 ml (7 fl oz)

*115 g (¾ cup) white sesame
  seeds
1-1½ tablespoons olive oil*

1. Toast sesame seeds in a dry hot frying pan, tossing, until golden.
2. Blend seeds and 2 tablespoons water with a hand-held blender for about 5–6 minutes until smooth and creamy. Add ½ teaspoon salt, adjusting to taste.
3. Place tahini in a jar with tight-fitting lid. Pour in oil to create a protective layer over the paste. Keeps refrigerated for about 2 months.

DUKKAH

makes 500 ml (2 cups)

100 g (3½ oz) nuts of your choosing, preferably with skin
2 tablespoons coriander seeds
1 tablespoon cumin seeds
1 teaspoon black peppercorns
75 g (½ cup) unhulled sesame seeds
1 tablespoon sea salt
1 tablespoon dried thyme

1. Preheat oven to 200°C (400°F).
2. Roast nuts for 10 minutes or until they begin to take on colour. Cool.
3. Toast coriander, cumin, and black pepper in a hot, dry frying pan for 2–3 minutes until fragrant.
4. Remove from heat and coarsely grind with a spice grinder or mortar and pestle. Transfer to a bowl.
5. Toast sesame seeds in a hot, dry frying pan, tossing, for 2–3 minutes until light golden. Add to bowl with spices.
6. Roughly chop nuts and add them to the other ingredients. Add salt and thyme and stir to combine.
7. Transfer to a glass jar with tight-fitting lid. Keeps for 2–3 months.

> Dukkah is usually made with hazel nuts, but you can be creative. Almond, pistachio, and pine nuts also work well. Dukkah brings a nice crunch to salads and can be used for crumbing—try doing it with white fish.

ZA'ATAR

makes 100 ml (3½ fl oz)

1 tablespoon sesame seeds
2 tablespoons dried thyme
1 tablespoons dried oregano
1 tablespoon ground sumac

1. Toast sesame seeds in a hot, dry frying pan, tossing, until golden.
2. Combine toasted sesame seeds with remaining ingredients and transfer to a jar with tight-fitting lid.

> Za'atar is a spice blend from the Middle East. As with most spice blends there are many different recipes, depending on the cook and their location. One version omits the sumac, for example. Za'atar is excellent on freshly baked bread, as a topping on hummus or labneh, or mixed with olive oil to make a marinade.

FURIKAKE

makes 200 ml (7 fl oz)
2 nori sheets
1 tablespoon dried wakame
2½ tablespoons white
   sesame seeds
2½ tablespoons black
   sesame seeds
1 tablespoon leek powder
   (page 124)

1. Toast the nori sheets in a hot, dry frying pan until they begin to darken and shrink slightly.
2. Cut the sheets into small pieces and place in a bowl.
3. Grind wakame and 1 tablespoon salt flakes to a powder with a spice grinder or mortar and pestle and combine with nori pieces.
4. Add sesame seeds and leek powder.
5. Transfer to a jar with tight-fitting lid.

> Furikake is a Japanese spice that tastes great sprinkled over most foods. It goes particularly well on rice, but you could also try coating raw salmon with it. After coating, slice the salmon thinly and serve it with Ponzu (page 59). Dried wakame (seaweed) is available from Asian grocers.

GOMASHIO

makes 100 ml (3½ fl oz)
60 g (2 oz) unhulled
   sesame seeds

1. Toast sesame seeds in a hot, dry frying pan until they take on a bit of colour and give off a nutty fragrance.
2. Let cool, then add 2 tablespoons salt flakes and grind to a coarse blend with a spice grinder or mortar and pestle.
3. Store in a jar with tight-fitting lid.

> Gomashio's nutty flavour makes it suitable as a topping for soups and salads. Try it on grilled eggplant or with meat and chicken. For a different spin, use black sesame seeds instead of white.

JERK SPICE

makes about 60 ml (2 fl oz)

1 cinnamon stick
3 teaspoons black
* peppercorns*
2 teaspoons allspice berries
1 tablespoon dried thyme
½ nutmeg kernel
1 dried red chilli

1. Toast cinnamon, black pepper, and allspice in a hot, dry frying pan, tossing, until fragrant.
2. Grind toasted spices together with thyme, nutmeg, and chilli in a spice or coffee grinder until you have a finely ground spice blend.

Jerk spice hails from the Caribbean, where it is used as a dry or wet rub. It's ideal as a dry rub for grilled chicken thighs or pork tenderloin.

BARBECUE RUB

makes 150 ml (5 fl oz)

2½ tablespoons smoky
* paprika*
2 tablespoons mild paprika
2 tablespoons raw sugar
½ teaspoon garlic powder
* (page 123)*
1 teaspoon onion powder
* (page 123)*

1. Combine all ingredients with 1 teaspoon salt and 1 teaspoon coarsely ground pepper in a bowl.
2. Store in a jar with tight-fitting lid.

FIVE-SPICE

makes about 60 ml (2 fl oz)

10 star anise
*3 teaspoons Sichuan
  peppercorns*
1 tablespoon fennel seeds
1 cinnamon stick
16 cloves

1. In a hot, dry frying pan, toast star anise, pepper, and fennel seeds on low heat until fragrant.
2. Grind the toasted spices together with cinnamon and cloves to a fine powder with a spice grinder or mortar and pestle.
3. Tastes best if used immediately, but if you want to save it, make sure to use a jar with tight-fitting lid.

> There are lots of different ways to make five-spice powder, but I'm fond of the wonderfully aromatic taste and the soft bite of the Sichuan pepper in this one. You could try adding ½ teaspoon ground ginger and 1 teaspoon ground coriander seeds for a rounder flavour profile. If you prefer an even milder blend, swap Sichuan pepper for the same amount of black pepper. Another variety is to make a flavourful salt by toasting 1 part five-spice and 4 parts salt in a hot, dry frying pan. Use it to season barbecued octopus or poached chicken.

TACO SPICE

makes 100 ml (3½ fl oz)

*1 tablespoon onion powder
  (page 123)*
1 tablespoon ground cumin
Pinch of dried chilli flakes
*Pinch of garlic powder
  (page 123)*
Pinch of leek ash (page 126)
1 tablespoon mild paprika
*1 teaspoon ground coriander
  seeds*
*1 teaspoon celery salt
  (page 129)*
1 teaspoon dried oregano

1. Combine all spices with 1 tablespoon salt.
2. Store in a jar with tight-fitting lid.

> This blend is delicious, incredibly simple and won't take more than a minute or two of your time. If the leek ash intimidates you, feel free to leave it out.

BOULLION POWDER

makes 100 ml (3½ fl oz)

2 brown onions, thinly sliced
2 tablespoons light soy
    sauce
⅓ leek, thinly sliced
½ celery stalk, thinly sliced
2 shiitake mushrooms,
    thinly sliced
3 tomatoes, thinly sliced

1. Place onion in a bowl and add soy. Marinate for 2 hours. Transfer to a sieve and press gently to remove most of the liquid.
2. Set oven to 55°C (130°F) or the lowest setting. Line a baking tray with baking paper and spread onion evenly on tray, or use a silicone sheet.
3. Spread leek, celery and mushrooms evenly on a separate lined tray, and tomato on another.
4. Place trays in oven to dry overnight. You might want to keep the oven door slightly ajar as tomatoes and onion contain a lot of liquid.
6. Grind dried vegetables to a fine powder with a mortar and pestle. Transfer to a jar with tight-fitting lid.

> This boullion powder is a real umami explosion and can easily replace store-bought boullion. Adds flavour to stews, soups, and sauces.

PORK SPICE

makes 100 ml (3½ fl oz)

2 tablespoons dried sage
1 teaspoon coarsely ground
    black pepper
3 pinches of dried chilli
    flakes
2 teaspoons leek ash
    (page 126)
1 teaspoon celery salt
    (page 129)
½ teaspoon dried lemon
    peel, crumbled
2 pinches of coarsely
    ground fennel seeds

1. Combine spices in a mortar with 2 teaspoons salt and grind to a coarse powder with a pestle. Store in a jar with tight-fitting lid.

> It's super easy to make the dried lemon peel required by this recipe. Just peel the outer layer of the lemon, careful to avoid the white part. Distribute the peels on a silicon sheet or a parchment paper and dry in oven at 50°C (120°F) or the lowest setting for 3 hours or overnight. Then grind to desired consistency with a mortar and pestle. Store in a cool and dark place. You can do this with other citrus fruits as well.

FISH SPICE

makes about 60 ml (2 fl oz)

1 tablespoon fennel seeds
2 dried juniper berries
5 pink peppercorns
1 teaspoon dried lemon peel
  (page 114)
½ teaspoon coarsely ground
  white pepper
½ teaspoon coarsely ground
  black pepper
1 tablespoon dried parsley
1 teaspoon celery salt
  (page 129)
1 teaspoon leek powder
  (page 124)
1 teaspoon faux celery salt
  (page 129)

1. Coarsely grind fennel, juniper berries, pink peppercorns, and lemon peel with a spice or coffee grinder.
2. Combine with remaining spices and transfer to a jar with tight-fitting lid.

> This spice blend is excellent with char-grilled fish. Mix it with a bit of oil and brush the fish with the blend throughout the cooking process.

CHICKEN SPICE

makes 100 ml (3½ fl oz)

3 tablespoons dried
  tarragon
3 tablespoons dried thyme
1 tablespoon onion powder
  (page 123)
2 tablespoons mild paprika
Pinch of dried chilli flakes
1½ teaspoons coarsely
  ground black pepper
1½ teaspoons coarsely
  ground white pepper
1½ teaspoons ground
  coriander seeds

1. Combine all ingredients with 1½ teaspoons salt and transfer to a jar with tight-fitting lid.

NORTH INDIAN CURRY POWDER

makes 100 ml (3½ fl oz)

2 teaspoons cumin seeds
1 teaspoon black mustard
   seeds
1 teaspoon fenugreek seeds
1 tablespoon coriander
   seeds
1 teaspoon black
   peppercorns
1 cinnamon stick, crushed
5 cloves
2 cardamom pods
1 dried red chilli, crushed
2 teaspoons ground
   turmeric
1 teaspoon ground ginger

1. Toast whole spices in a hot, dry frying pan, tossing, for 2–3 minutes until fragrant.
2. Grind toasted spices together with chilli and ground spices with a spice grinder to make a fine powder.
3. Transfer to a glass jar with tight-fitting lid. Store at room temperature out of direct sunlight.

GARAM MASALA

makes 100 ml (3½ fl oz)

2 tablespoons coriander
   seeds
1 tablespoon cumin seeds
2 teaspoon black
   peppercorns
1 teaspoon cardamom pods
1 teaspoon fennel seeds
½ teaspoon cloves
2 teaspoons black mustard
   seeds
½ teaspoon fenugreek seeds
3 dried bay leaves
Pinch of ground nutmeg
½ cinnamon stick

1. Toast spices, except for bay leaves, nutmeg, and cinnamon, in a hot, dry frying pan until fragrant.
2. Grind toasted spices with remaining ingredients in a spice grinder to make a fine powder.
3. Transfer spice blend to a glass jar with a tight-fitting lid. Store at room temperature out of direct sunlight.

GREEN CURRY PASTE

makes 150 ml (5 fl oz)

*1 tablespoon ground
  coriander seeds*
15 white peppercorns
2 green bird's-eye chillies
*50 g (about 15) small red
  Asian shallots*
3 garlic cloves
*1 handful chopped coriander
  (cilantro) with roots*
*1 x 6 cm (2½ in) piece
  galangal*
½ tablespoon dried shrimp
4 kaffir lime leaves
*1 lemongrass stem, pale
  part only*
2 tablespoons neutral oil

1. Toast dry spices in a hot, dry frying pan until fragrant.
   Crush with a mortar and pestle.
2. Roughly chop remaining ingredients and pound to
   a paste with ground spices.
3. Transfer curry paste to a sterilised jar with tight-fitting lid.
   Keeps refrigerated for about 2 weeks.

Green curry paste is probably most commonly used with
coconut milk in soups and stews. But I find this fragrant paste
an excellent marinade for chicken, pork, and seafood—you
might use oil or coconut milk to thin it. Or rub it on a whole
fish before barbecuing or roasting it in the oven. Serve with rice,
a bright salad and a bunch of Asian herbs. Galangal, shrimp
paste and kaffir lime leaves are available from Asian grocers.

YELLOW CURRY PASTE

makes 150 ml (5 fl oz)

*1 teaspoon white
  peppercorns*
½ teaspoon cumin seeds
1 teaspoon coriander seeds
1 teaspoon curry powder
*1 x 3 cm (1¼ in) piece ginger,
  peeled and coarsely
  chopped*
*1 x 3 cm (1¼ in) piece
  galangal, peeled and
  coarsely chopped*
*1 x 3 cm (1¼ in) piece
  turmeric, rinsed and
  coarsely chopped*
*1–2 red bird's-eye chillies,
  coarsely chopped*
*50 g (1¾ oz; about 15) small
  red Asian shallots, coarsely
  chopped*
*4 garlic cloves, coarsely
  chopped*
*1 lemongrass stem, pale part
  only, coarsely chopped*
½ teaspoon shrimp paste
1 tablespoon neutral oil

1. Begin by toasting the dry spices in a hot, dry frying
   pan until fragrant.
2. Combine all ingredients in a food processor with
   1 teaspoon salt and blend to a paste.
3. Transfer to a sterilised glass jar. Keeps refrigerated for
   about 3 weeks.

Yellow curry paste is a fairly mild and fragrant spice paste that's
a staple in Southeast Asian cooking. It gets its yellow colour
from fresh turmeric. Nice in curries with a coconut milk base,
but also with tomato bases. It's particularly good in fish and
seafood curries. Galangal, turmeric and shrimp paste are
available from Asian grocers.

Green curry paste

CONFIT GARLIC PASTE
& GARLIC OIL

**makes about 300 ml
(10½ fl oz) garlic oil and
about 100 ml (3½ fl oz)
garlic paste**
2 garlic bulbs
300 ml (10½ fl oz) canola oil

1. Separate and peel garlic cloves.
2. Heat oil to 100–110°C (200–225°F) in a heavy-based saucepan.
3. Add garlic and simmer for about 15 minutes or until the cloves are very soft.
4. Remove garlic from oil with a slotted spoon. Allow oil to cool slightly, then pour into a sterilised bottle.
5. Combine garlic and ½ teaspoon salt and blend to a smooth purée with a hand-held blender. Transfer to a sterilised jar with tight-fitting lid.
6. Confit garlic paste and oil will keep refrigerated for about 2 months.

> Fresh garlic can be a little sharp for some recipes. In those cases, garlic oil and garlic confit paste are ideal for adding a mild and deep, almost sweet garlic flavour to marinades, salsa, and sauces. The oil is excellent for frying mushrooms and green beans, or as an ingredient in aioli.

TRUFFLE TAPENADE

makes 100 ml (3½ fl oz)
*5 porcini mushrooms, very
   finely chopped*
2 teaspoons light soy sauce
*¼ teaspoon mushroom
   powder (page 124)*
2 teaspoons truffle oil

1. Combine mushrooms with remaining ingredients in a bowl.
2. Transfer mixture to a sterilised jar and let sit for 1 hour or so before serving. Keeps refrigerated for about 2 weeks.

> Raw mushrooms combined with truffle oil and soy sauce have a nice umami flavour and provide a good substitute when you don't want to use real truffle. The tapenade goes well with pasta, in sauces and dips, or in truffle mayonnaise.

ONION POWDER

makes 100 ml (3½ fl oz)

*6 brown onions, thinly sliced
with a mandoline*

1. Preheat oven to 55°C (130°F) or the lowest setting.
2. Spread sliced onion on a baking tray lined with baking paper or a silicone sheet and place on oven rack. Leave in the oven overnight until the onion is completely dry.
3. Grind dried onion to a fine powder with a spice or coffee grinder.
4. Store powder in a jar with tight-fitting lid.

GARLIC POWDER

makes 100 ml (3½ fl oz)

5 garlic bulbs

1. Preheat oven to 55°C (130°F) or the lowest setting.
2. Separate and peel garlic cloves. Slice thinly with a mandoline or a sharp knife.
3. Spread garlic on a baking tray lined with baking paper or a silicone sheet and place on oven rack. Leave in the oven overnight until the garlic is completely dry.
4. Grind to a fine powder with a spice or coffee grinder.
5. Store powder in a jar with tight-fitting lid.

> Heads up! Both onion and garlic need to be completely dry when you grind them, or you'll end up with clumps and a less fine powder. Every oven is different and you might need to keep the door of yours slightly ajar for the best results. This is easily done with a wooden spoon. If you don't have a silicone sheet, baking trays work just as well, but you might need to extend the drying period a bit.

LEEK POWDER

makes 100 ml (3½ fl oz)
3 leeks

1. Preheat oven to 55°C (130°F) or the lowest setting.
2. Rinse leeks and cut off root and dark green top parts. Then cut in quarters lengthwise.
3. Spread leek on a baking tray lined with baking paper or a silicone sheet and place on oven rack. Leave in the oven overnight until completely dry.
4. Grind leeks to a fine powder with a spice grinder or a mortar and pestle.
5. Store powder in a jar with tight-fitting lid.

MUSHROOM POWDER

makes 100 ml (3½ fl oz)
175 g (6 oz) fresh mushrooms (such as shiitake or porcini), brushed clean

1. Preheat oven to 55°C (130°F) or the lowest setting.
2. Spread mushroom on a baking tray lined with baking paper or a silicone sheet and place on oven rack. Leave in the oven overnight until completely dry.
3. Grind dried mushrooms to a fine powder with a spice grinder or mortar and pestle.
4. Store powder in a jar with tight-fitting lid.

> The mushroom powder can be made with most types of mushrooms, but I find that shiitake or porcini yield the best flavour. Use the powder in broths, sauces, and risottos, where its mushroom flavour gives a nice jolt of umami.

PERSILLADE

makes 100 ml (3½ fl oz)
1 handful dried parsley, crumbled
2 pinches of garlic powder (page 123)
2 teaspoons chopped dried shallots

1. Combine all ingredients and transfer to jar with a tight-fitting lid.

> This recipe calls for chopped, dried shallots. Make them by thinly slicing shallots and drying them in a low oven overnight as per the onion powder recipe on page 123.

HERBES DE PROVENCE

makes 500 ml (17 fl oz)
*1 handful dried summer
  savoury (or sage)*
1 handful dried rosemary
1 handful dried thyme
*1 small handful dried
  oregano*
1 teaspoon dried basil

1. Combine all herbs in a bowl. Transfer to a jar with tight-fitting lid.

SALAD SPICE

makes 100 ml (3½ fl oz)
*1½ tablespoon celery salt
  (page 129)*
*1 tablespoon leek powder
  (page 124)*
*1½ teaspoons onion powder
  (page 123)*
*3 pinches of garlic powder
  (page 123)*
1 tablespoon dried parsley
1½ teaspoons dried oregano
1 tablespoon dried chives

1. Use a spice grinder or mortar and pestle to grind all spices into a fine powder.
2. Transfer to a jar with tight-fitting lid.

HERB SALT

makes 200 ml (7 fl oz)
*1 teaspoon leek powder
  (page 124)*
3 tablespoons dried chives
3 tablespoons dried parsley
1 teaspoon dried tarragon
1 teaspoon dried marjoram
*2 tablespoons celery salt
  (page 129)*
50 g (1¾ oz) salt flakes

1. Pound herbs with a mortar and pestle until combined. Add both types of salt and pound to combine.
2. Transfer to a jar with tight-fitting lid.

LEEK ASH

makes 100 ml (3½ fl oz)

3 leeks

1. Preheat the oven grill (broiler) to 230°C (450°F).
2. Trim leeks by cutting off roots and dark green parts.
3. Quarter the leeks lengthwise and place on a baking tray.
4. Grill (broil) leeks until fully black, about 15 minutes. You may need to turn them over to get them black on both sides.
5. Cool, then grind to a fine powder with a mortar and pestle or spice grinder.
6. Transfer to a jar with tight-fitting lid. Keeps forever.

GRILLING OIL

makes 100 ml (3½ fl oz)

2 tablespoons leek ash (above)
100 ml (3½ fl oz) high-quality olive oil

1. Combine ash and oil and pour into sterilised jar with tight-fitting lid.
2. Store at room temperature. Keeps for at least 1 year.

> This oil is not primarily meant for grilling, but rather for giving a grilled taste to food. Try it on a piece of sashimi, for example. It's also perfect if you're having barbecue cravings in the dead of winter but don't keep the barbecue out year round.

ASH SALT

makes 200 ml (7 fl oz)

50 g (1¾ oz) salt flakes, preferably Fleur de sel Guérande
1 teaspoon leek ash (above)

1. Carefully mix salt and ash with your hands to combine.
2. Pour into a jar with tight-fitting lid. Keeps more or less forever.

SICILIAN SPICE SALT

makes 100 ml (3½ fl oz)
*1 teaspoon dried juniper
  berries*
1 teaspoon fennel seeds
*1 teaspoon dried orange
  peel (page 114)*
2 teaspoons dried rosemary
½ teaspoon chilli flakes
*½ teaspoon celery salt
  (below)*
25 g (1 oz) salt flakes

1. Coarsely crush juniper berries, fennel seeds and orange peel with a mortar and pestle.
2. Add remaining ingredients and stir to combine.
3. Transfer to a jar with tight-fitting lid.

CELERY SALT

makes 100 ml (3½ fl oz)
1 tablespoon celery seeds
25 g (1 oz) salt flakes

1. In a hot, dry frying pan, toast celery seeds, tossing, for 1 minute or so until fragrant. Be careful not to burn them.
2. Coarsely grind celery seeds with a mortar and pestle.
3. Add salt and continue grinding until a fine salt.
4. Transfer to a jar with tight-fitting lid.

> Celery salt is a good flavour booster and works well in many recipes. Try adding it to a minced meat sauce or a Bloody Mary. Or use it to season lobster tails, fry them and serve them with gazpacho.

FAUX CELERY SALT

makes 100 ml (3½ fl oz)
*1 celery stalk, thinly sliced
  on a mandoline*
25 g (1 oz) salt flakes

1. Preheat oven to 55°C (130°F) or the lowest setting.
2. Spread celery on a baking tray lined with baking paper or a silicone sheet and place on oven rack. Leave in the oven overnight until completely dry.
3. Finely grind celery and salt with a mortar and pestle to a fine salt. Store in a jar with tight-fitting lid.

> I couldn't find the celery seeds used for celery salt, so instead I tried combining salt with dried celery. It doesn't have the same character as 'real' celery salt, but still tastes great. It's particularly nice in recipes with seafood or tomato. Or try mixing it with sour cream and onion powder to make a dip.

Faux celery salt, gomashio, herb salt,
celery salt, Sicilian spice salt and ash salt.

TOOLS AND TRICKS

You don't really need any special tools to make the recipes in this book. But a few things are helpful to have on hand, and others are good to keep in mind.

Weighing and measuring
Ingredients are often measured by weight, which is more precise than volume. A kitchen scale is a good investment that's low-cost and high-gain. It will make your measurements more exact, and also results in fewer dishes to wash—just put one container on the scales and reset the tare after each new ingredient.

Jars and bottles
I use glass jars and glass bottles almost exclusively. They are more durable than other materials and can be machine washed over and over again. Moreover, glass doesn't take on colour and scent. I usually repurpose old jars and bottles, which works great as long as the lids are tight-fitting. I also keep an eye out for relatively small bottles and jars, preferring many small containers to one large. That's mainly because I like to give condiments to friends, but this approach also extends shelf life since you'll finish a small jar faster than a big one. A condiment will go bad much faster once you've opened the lid, and especially if you put your finger or a dirty spoon in the jar.

Fermentation
Many of the recipes in this book require some type of fermentation. This happens best in large glass jars without lids, as the process requires oxygen. Use a piece of fabric instead of a lid to keep dirt and flies at bay. Most types of fabric, from old sheets to a piece of muslin (cheesecloth), work well.

Ideal fermentation occurs at 18-22°C (65–72°F) degrees, out of direct sunlight and with plenty of oxygen. Unfortunately, fermentation of something like vinegar is a fruit fly's dream, and these creatures love to flock around the jars. Jars which, by the way, have a tendency to smell a little. But these are the kinds of punches you have to roll with when you make your own condiments. And if you want to become the lord of the fruit flies the internet is full of tips on how to get rid of them.

> **Tools pictured:**
> *Spice grinder/coffee grinder*
> *Disposable gloves*
> *Hand-held blender + chopper*
> *Funnel*
> *Sieve*
> *Mortar and pestle*
> *Glass jar with tight-fitting lid*
> *Rubber band and piece of fabric*
> *Digital kitchen scale*
> *Measuring cups*

Blending and grinding

Many of these recipes involve some blending or grinding. You'll get a long way with a mortar and pestle and a hand-held blender. I often use an electric spice grinder (it's probably meant as a coffee grinder), which is great for grinding spices, from nutmeg to coriander seeds.

A blender attachment is a useful addition to the hand blender when you make wet spice pastes, and a blender is useful for larger quantities of liquid, like hot sauce.

In recipes that call for a really smooth consistency, and where the sauce is going to be passed through a sieve, I recommend a long blending time. My rule of thumb: when you think you're done blending, keep going for double the time. Otherwise you risk losing some of the flavour and having a coarse consistency.

Shelf life and storage

Throughout, I recommend using sterilised bottles and jars. There are a few different cleaning methods: run them on high heat in a dishwasher, convection steam oven, regular oven, or pressure cooker. You can wash them carefully by hand, or even boil them in a pot on the stove. But if you want to make sure your glass jars and bottles are truly sterilised, bake them in the oven at 100°C (200°F) for 30 minutes. Any bacteria will die, and the risk that something starts growing in your condiment is highly reduced. Don't forget to clean or sterilise the lids too. With hot condiments, simply turn the jar upside down for a few moments to sterilise the lid. I usually sterilise bottles and jars when I'm making a big batch of something I want a long shelf life for. Otherwise I think it's enough to wash them carefully in hot water.

Opened jars and bottles tend to do best in the fridge, as cold temperature extends shelf life. But unopened bottles keep well as long as they're stored in a cool, dark place. You can extend the shelf life of a lot of foods by pasteurising them. Heat the bottles and jars with their condiments inside to more than 70°C (150°F) degrees for 10 minutes, and most bacteria will die.

There are no perfect rules when it comes to shelf life. You'll have to trust your senses—if it smells and tastes good, it's usually fine to eat.

INGREDIENT GLOSSARY, A-Z

Bonito flakes
Flakes of dried, smoked bonito. Bonito flakes, or katsuobushi as they are called in Japanese, are central in the dashi broth used for miso soup. Nice as a topping on sushi or okonomiyaki.

Chinkiang vinegar
Chinese black rice vinegar made from sticky rice with a soft, acidic taste. Tasty mixed with soy sauce for dumplings, or sprinkled over poached chicken with rice and some chilli oil. You'll find it in well-stocked Asian grocery stores.

Doenjang
Miso's Korean, slightly gruffer, cousin. A thick, coarse chilli paste made from fermented soy beans and salt. Gives a jolt of umami to sauces, dips, stews, and soups.

Fermented black beans
Black Chinese beans that more closely resemble the droppings from some little rodent than something you'd eat. A staple in the Chinese kitchen that provides an explosion of flavour. If they're too salty for you, rinse and chop finely to soften.

Galangal
A cousin of ginger, but much harder and more woody. Its flavour is more peppery and perfumed, and it's central to Thai curry recipes and in many Asian spice pastes.

Gochujang
A thick, red paste made from chilli pepper, sticky rice, fermented soy beans, and salt. The flavour is spicy, sweet, and hot. A staple in the Korean kitchen and often served with bibimbap.

Kaffir lime
A small, green lime fruit with lumpy peel. Hard and compact, and contains almost no juice. Instead you use the peel, which has a characteristic fragrant flavour. The leaves are somewhat more commonly found than the fruit—most Asian grocery stores stock them. The fresh leaves are in a whole different league to the dried variety.

Gochugaru
Korean dried chilli powder, most commonly sold as flakes. Used primarily in kimchi.

Kombu
A type of kelp. It grows fast and gets really tall. Used primarily in dashi broth, but can also be ground for spice blends.

Maple syrup
Most commonly made from the sap of the sugar maple, it has a rich, sweet, slight caramel flavour. Avoid golden or pancake syrup and make sure you get real maple syrup.

Molasses
Molasses is a by-product of sugar production. A thick, black syrup that's got a rich flavour with notes of dark caramel and liquorice. I prefer sugarcane molasses and black-strap molasses to other varieties. You can find it in well-stocked health food stores and with sellers of British or American goods.

Miso paste
Japanese fermented soy paste. Packed with umami, and one of the main ingredients in miso soup. I tend to use white miso, also known as shiro miso. Its flavour is mild and soft with a perfect saltiness, and it has a wide variety of uses. Try it in ramen, broths, salad dressings and sauces.

Mirin
A type of rice wine with high sugar content, which in true mirin occurs naturally in the fermentation process. True mirin is also called hon-mirin and has an alcohol level of 14%. The type of mirin most commonly found, however, is free from alcohol and has a lot of added sugar, but it still works great in recipes.

Nigella seeds
Seeds from the nigella plant have a nutty, peppery and slightly bitter taste. Most commonly used in Indian recipes and in food from the Middle East. Also called black caraway and black cumin. Commonly strewn over naan bread and used in many different types of chutney.

Nori sheets
Made from pressed and toasted red algae. Sold as sheets, flakes, and thin strips.

Palm sugar
Extracted from the sap of the palm tree and a frequent ingredient in Asian recipes. Sold in Asian grocery stores in the shape of little disks or rectangles. They are really hard, so I make sure to use a good grater.

Rice vinegar
A staple all over Asia and sold in many different colours and types. I recommend the Japanese kind, which has a soft, less sharp taste.

Shrimp paste
Thai shrimp paste made from fermented shrimps and salt. Has a very particular scent. Gives depth to Thai recipes, curries, and spice pastes.

Sake
Japanese alcoholic drink made from polished rice.

Sesame seeds, unhulled
As the name indicates, these seeds still have their hulls. They're slightly tougher than the hulled variety, and have a nuttier character.

Tamarind paste
Made from tamarind fruit, with a distinctly sour flavour.

Turmeric
Part of the ginger family. You'll find fresh turmeric in Asian grocery stores, or well-stocked health food stores. The taste is slightly bitter, but quite sharp and peppery. Often used in curry paste. Be careful, as it dyes everything it touches yellow!

Unhomogenised milk
The homogenisation process cuts all fat molecules and makes them uniform in size, which means they don't rise to the surface. With unhomogenised milk, the biggest fat molecules rise to the surface, creating a layer of cream on top.

Whey
When milk is curdled and strained, whey it was remains. It's rich in enzymes and living bacteria, which makes it an excellent starter for fermenting foods using lactic acid.

Wakame
A mild-tasting Japanese brown seaweed. Nice in salads and miso soup.

Yuzu juice
Yuzu is an East Asian citrus fruit with a highly aromatic juice. Fresh yuzu can sometimes be hard to find, but the bottled juice can often be found in Asian grocery stores and other well-stocked grocers.

ACKNOWLEDGMENTS

This book would never have happened if Matilda hadn't loved the idea and worked with Karin and Karolina to help shape my thoughts into a book concept. I'm forever indebted to them. Nor would the book have looked as good with all these magical photographs were it not for Matilda. Thank you for your energy, your imaginative mind, and for giving the book its coherent identity. That you've dealt with my 'creative' chaos brain for more than a year is quite an accomplishment. I'd also like to express my gratitude to Lina, the best photography assistant we could have asked for. Thank you for your invaluable help, and for always being willing and ready to hunt down unusual spices and perfect-looking plums.

   Thank you Mikael, for giving the book its gorgeous look by bringing your skilful consideration to each of its elements.

   Thanks to Lhådös kakel for generously donating the tiles used in photographs throughout the book. .

   Thank you Zvonko for your invaluable expertise in all things food-related.

   Huge thanks to my family and friends, who constantly encourage and support me in things both large and small.

   And an equally enormous thanks to Elisabeth, the world's best editor, and Maria, the world's best publisher, for your expansive knowledge and phenomenal enthusiasm for this project. Writing my first cookbook under your wings has been a true honour.

Finally I want to thank Filip, for believing in me and giving me the self-confidence I often lack myself. Thank you for not complaining a single time during this project, not even when we found sriracha splatter in the ceiling, had a colony of fruit flies as squatters, or lived and breathed fermented chilli for more than a year. Becoming your wife is bigger than everything.

INDEX

Italicised number = photo page

Published in 2020 by Murdoch Books, an imprint of Allen & Unwin
First published in 2015 by Natur & Kultur, Sweden

Murdoch Books Australia
83 Alexander Street
Crows Nest NSW 2065
Phone: +61 (0) 2 8425 0100
murdochbooks.com.au
info@murdochbooks.com.au

Murdoch Books UK
Ormond House, 26–27 Boswell Street
London WC1N 3JZ
Phone: +44 (0) 20 8785 5995
murdochbooks.co.uk
info@murdochbooks.co.uk

For corporate orders & custom publishing, contact our business
development team at salesenquiries@murdochbooks.com.au

Design: Mikael Engblom
Photography: Matilda Lindeblad
Editor: Elisabeth Fock
Prepress: Turbin

Publisher: Corinne Roberts
Translator: Kira Josefsson
English-language editor: David Matthews

ISBN 978 1 76052 540 8 Australia
ISBN 978 1 91163 260 3 UK

A catalogue record for this book
is available from the National
Library of Australia

A catalogue record for this book is available from the British Library

Printed by C & C Offset Printing Co. Ltd., China

The paper in this book is FSC® certified.
FSC® promotes environmentally responsible,
socially beneficial and economically viable
management of the world's forests.